RADIO BLACK

SAFFRON

SANDRIFT

WALNUT

TEAK

GW01281136

Fifties Furniture
by Paul McCobb
Directional Designs

Preface by Jennifer A. Lindbeck
Value Guide by Leslie Piña and Michael Ellison

Schiffer Publishing Ltd

4880 Lower Valley Road, Atglen, PA 19310 USA

Preface and Value Guide Copyright © 2000 by Schiffer Publishing Ltd.
Copyright © 1956 by Directional Furniture Showrooms Incorporated

Library of Congress Catalog Card Number: 99-69930

All rights reserved. No part of this work may be reproduced or used in any form or by any means—graphic, electronic, or mechanical, including photocopying or information storage and retrieval systems—without written permission from the copyright holder.
"Schiffer," "Schiffer Publishing Ltd. & Design," and the "Design of pen and ink well" are registered trademarks of Schiffer Publishing Ltd.

Type set in ZapfCalligr BT/ZapfHumnst BT

ISBN: 0-7643-1139-5
Printed in China

Published by Schiffer Publishing Ltd.
4880 Lower Valley Road
Atglen, PA 19310
Phone: (610) 593-1777; Fax: (610) 593-2002
E-mail: Schifferbk@aol.com
Please visit our web site catalog at www.schifferbooks.com

In Europe, Schiffer books are distributed by Bushwood Books
6 Marksbury Avenue Kew Gardens
Surrey TW9 4JF England
Phone: 44 (0)208-392-8585; Fax: 44 (0)208-392-9876
E-mail: Bushwd@aol.com
Free postage in the UK. Europe: air mail at cost.

This book may be purchased from the publisher.
Include $3.95 for shipping. Please try your bookstore first.
We are always looking for people to write books on new and related subjects.
If you have an idea for a book, please contact us at the address above.
You may write for a free catalog.

DIRECTIONAL DESIGNS / PAUL McCOBB

Preface

by Jennifer A. Lindbeck

Paul McCobb's designs for furniture and interiors have far surpassed today's appeals for a retro look and become classic.

Born in 1917, in Boston, Massachusetts, McCobb first trained as an artist/painter, studying at the Vester School of Fine Arts. At twenty, he was hired by the Boston department store, Jordan Marsh, to work as a display and store interior designer. Through his interaction with decorators and consumers, he gained early on a fundamental knowledge of decorating, and its mechanical aspects, and of the needs and tastes involved in furnishing New England homes. Following an Army stint during World War II, McCobb moved to New York where, by the late 1940s, he had successfully established himself as a furniture designer—first working as a product development engineer in the plastics industry, then as an associate in an industrial design office, and, in 1945, forming his own industrial design company, Paul McCobb Design Associates. Pairing up with New York furniture distributor B.G. Mersberg, McCobb went on to develop a line of furniture and interiors known as the Planner Group, which was introduced to the public in January of 1950.

The post-war climate of the late '40s and early '50s had created a great desire for durable, affordable, and functional furnishings to be put within arm's reach of consumers. To give some indication of the environment for design during this period, the Museum of Modern Art in New York held the "International Competition for Low-Cost Furniture Design" in 1948. Objectives for the competition included designs for "furniture that is adaptable to small apartments and houses . . . well-designed yet moderate in price . . . easily moved, stored, [and] furniture that is planned and executed to fit the needs of modern living" (Hiesinger and Marcus, 152). Incentives such as this only further encouraged the development of "low-cost" designs and their subsequent introduction into the consumer market.

Given consumers' needs for furniture to serve for a variety of purposes in the home and furniture designed to last, circumstances proved ideal for McCobb's low-cost Planner Group. This simple, functional line, made from birch and maple, became known for its "sleek simplicity" (Ritter, 19). The modular furniture components and storage units, which included chairs, tables, benches, and shelves, were designed to be placed individually in the home or to be combined for maximum use and versatility. A bench, for example, could be used for seating but also might serve as a coffee table or a base upon which to place a storage unit (Ritter). Units for the line also came with interchangeable interiors. This same concept can be seen in some of McCobb's designs for the Directional Group, seen herein. Upholstered pieces were added shortly after the line's introduction. Planner Group designs experienced success on the American market, but also abroad, being retailed and manufactured for distribution in Europe, Canada, Cuba, and Puerto Rico. Designs from McCobb's Planner Group earned a reputation as "furniture of the people," and advertisements for the line heralded that it was "hard to conceive of a problem in today's living that cannot be solved with this moderately priced furniture" (Ricapito).

Following the success of the Planner Group, McCobb developed other lines, which included the Directional (shown here), Predicator, Irwin, Perimeter, Linear, and Delineator. The Directional Group targeted a higher-end market, utilizing more elaborate materials like walnut and brass. Exclusive showrooms for the line had locations in New York, Chicago, and Los Angeles, with various Directional designs featured in showrooms in Atlanta, Boston, Buffalo, Cleveland, Dallas, Grand Rapids, Kansas City, Miami, Milwaukee, Minneapolis, Pittsburgh, San Fransisco, and St. Louis. Despite the slight shift in consumer appeal, designs for the Directional Group also followed the principle that "designers must design for people and their needs."

In addition to furniture of all kinds, McCobb's design lines included fabrics, wallpapers, lamps, ashtrays, candelabras, glasswares, dishes, ceramics, metalware, television sets, plant stands, watches, clocks, and even typewriters for Remington. He created modular storage systems known as "living walls," as well as introduced the use of metal in home furnishings (Moritz, 469).

Because affordable prices were a primary consideration in McCobb's work, Americans easily furnished their homes and interior spaces with his designs. His training as an industrial engineer enabled him to approach ideas for design from a mechanical standpoint. All aspects—strength, durability, cost of materials, and construction—were weighed in the execution of his designs. He made sure he was well briefed on the various ways a piece could be fashioned, personally working out the details for assemblage. He knew, for example, that furniture legs could be square, turned, joints could be dovetailed, doweled, or screwed, and that lumber is made available in standardized sizes (sizes that deviate from the standard result in a cost increase). However, good design was not sacrificed to low costs, according to McCobb (Ritter). Ultimately, his decisions for design rested on his aim to make furniture an affordable and "lasting commodity" ("Paul McCobb,..." *The New York Times*), which, as noted, directly appealed to the needs and tastes of mid century consumers.

McCobb's philosophy on design and his previous training as an industrial engineer also had bearing on his success. He believed "the contemporary room [should be] fairly cleanly designed" and that the furniture in it "should properly remain quiet and serve as a background for those who live with it" (Ritter). He had a clear desire to create furniture with a permanence of beauty and utility. He used traditional forms as the basis for his designs, which also show an influence of Scandinavian craftsmanship and the styles of Windsor, Shaker, neo-classical, and neo-traditional. His designs had an "it's-all-you-need" (Ricapito) appeal that attracted many consumers of the day.

McCobb's Planner Group remains one of his most popular furniture lines and was the top seller in contemporary furniture during the 1960s America (Hiesinger and Marcus, 169). His many awards, merits, and contributions also testify to his success as a pioneer in mid twentieth-century furniture and interiors designs. His designs were shown at numerous exhibitions and fairs, in the United States and abroad. He received the Good Design Award from the Museum of Modern Art five times from 1950 1955; multiple awards from the Hardwood Institute—the Industrial Product Award and their annual award for furniture design in 1953, 195 and 1958; the Contribution to Better Design Award from the Philadelphia Museum of Art in 1959; The Home Fashions League Trail Blazers Award in 1953; the Design in Steel Award in 1964; and the Massachusetts Industries Annual Design Award in 1965. He also offered design consultation some leading mid century companies, including Columbia Records, the Singer Manufacturing Company, the Bell & Howell Company, Alcoa, the Goodyear Tire and Rubber Company, the Philco Corporation, a Remington Rand.

McCobb's designs were a ready staple in many American homes. His ability to provide a large segment of the consumer market with serviceable, functional, lasting furniture at an affordable cost earned him the title "America's decorator" (Ricapito). Despite the ubiquitous placement McCobb furniture designs had in homes of the mid twentieth-century amidst the background of everyday living, today they are regarded as backbone for classic, modern design.

References

Hiesinger, Kathryn B. & George H. Marcus. *Landmarks of Twentieth-Century Design: An Illustrated Handbook*. New York: Abbeville, 1993.

Landee, Marjorie Dent. "McCobb, Paul (Winthrop)." *Current Biography Yearbook 1958*. New York, New York: The H.W. Wilson Company, 1958.

"McCobb, Paul (Winthrop)." *Who Was Who in America with World Notables* v. 5 (1969-1973). Chicago, Illinois: Marquis Who's Who, Inc., 1973.

Moritz, Charles, ed. "McCobb, Paul (Winthrop)." *Current Biography Yearbook 1969*. New York, New York: The H. W. Wilson Company, 1969, 1970.

O.G. "McCobb's Predictor." *Interiors* 111 (October 1951): p. 126-29.

"Paul McCobb, Modern Designer, Dies." *The New York Times*, 12 March 196 p. 33.

Pile, John. *Dictionary of 20th-Century Design*. New York, New York: Facts File, 1990.

Piña, Leslie. *Fifties Furniture*. Revised and Expanded 2nd Edition. Atgle Pennsylvania: Schiffer Publishing Ltd., 1999.

Ricapito, Maria. "1950's Hallmarks, Modern but Well Mannered." *The New York Times*, 20 June 1996: C2.

Ritter, Chris. "An Interior View." *Art Digest* 26 (September 1952): p. 19.

Paul McCobb

CONTEMPORARY DESIGN today is serving the needs of the people and improving the usefulness and esthetic forms of their objects. It has its roots in the growth of a new awareness of the inter-relationships of human activities. In all epochs in which creative work has been produced, it has given us an intellectual and artistic perspective of a culture. History is not simply a repository of unchanging facts but a process, a pattern of living and changing attitudes and interpretations. With this thought in mind, we are able to look at that which is representative of the past, and accept those designs which have proven to be classics of their times, and understand what aspects of them are meaningful today. A period should be understood comprehensively: its architecture, painting and sculpture, its products and tools, as well as the social structure in which these develop.

A designer must be a keen observer of his own period, interested and aware of all aspects of his times, the economic and social structures, particularly the arts and sciences. Contemporary design, like modern science, recognizes the fact that observation, and what is observed, form one complex situation — to observe is to act upon and to alter. A designer is constantly striving to express his point of view in the form of designs best suited to contemporary needs.

Aware of the historical context of his work, today's designer must design directly for the people, recognizing their needs, wants and aspirations. The human being is the final element that makes a design work or not work — every design must be carefully engineered to work properly and to have that intangible extra interest that develops a desire for possession. It becomes an intimate part of everyday life, making it more pleasant, meaningful and rewarding. This process in turn establishes the receptive climate in which a designer is able to produce his most creative work.

All contemporary design must be based on the sincere application of the fundamental qualities of good design: creative concepts, honest use of materials, efficient and intelligent use of advanced production techniques, exacting proportions and details — achieving an overall integrity of product.

A designer capable of maintaining this high level of approach, inevitably helps to raise the standard of living and culture of a people, and possibly leaves a heritage which may parallel or even excel the great achievements of the past.

8

CONTENTS

Introduction	5
Storage	15
Dining	39
Occasional furniture and tables	47
Bedroom	69
Seating	77
Desks	101
Index Specifications	107

26 24" CABINET, **7023** 36" BAR CABINET, **7025** 24" CHEST. WALNUT FINISH, BRASS LEG POSTS / BAR HAS LIFT-UP TOP, WHITE MICARTA WELL / 402 CHAIR.

THIS COMPREHENSIVE VOLUME has two objectives, first to present the full scope of Paul McCobb's Directional Collection, and second to show the design philosophy underlining his concept of a contemporary design indigenous to this country and its living needs. His philosophy is inherent in his designs and evident here in the exacting proportions, refined details, careful selection of structural materials, superior craftsmanship, and an overall integration which permits complete coordination of all units.

An unerring sense of proportion characterizes all of Paul McCobb's designs and creates a distinctive elegance and simplicity. The esthetic result denotes an individual taste which has already become a permanent contribution to a developing American culture.

Paul McCobb firmly believes in the architectural relatedness of furniture to the interior space it will occupy. His work is conceived in the context of three dimensional space. It evolves first from an abstract conception of spatial interrelationships through development and experimentation to the final product, keeping line, material, scale, detail and production techniques, in perfect harmony with each other.

Although this book concerns itself solely with the Directional Furniture Collection, Paul McCobb's design virtuosity extends to other important furniture groups, as well as fabrics, lighting fixtures, hi-fidelity and television units and many other consumer products, all completely contemporary in concept. His design eminence is acknowledged by the presence of his work in many museum collections as well as awards granted him in national and international design competitions.

As the level of American taste rises, well designed contemporary products by designers such as Paul McCobb are accepted as an integral part of our culture, reflected in our homes, institutions and places of business. This volume is dedicated to the advancement of this purpose.

THE DIRECTIONAL FURNITURE COLLECTION is the product of a progressive design program directed by Paul McCobb, to create contemporary home furnishings in the best tradition of the earlier noteworthy American artisans.

As we look at the works of illustrious designers of the past we cannot fail to observe the genius that endows their products with the permanent qualities of beauty and utility. Through the exquisite use of materials, superb craftsmanship, grace and proportion, Paul McCobb has avoided the ephemeral and the bizarre by his adherence to these lasting principles of good design.

The collection is the handiwork of several of the finest furniture factories in America, each uniquely equipped to make a part of the line using the finest techniques and skills of the industry. Directional Furniture is strongly influenced by the methods and principles of the furniture craftsman. This influence on the plants manufacturing the Directional Collection is evident in the specialized handicraft techniques of caning, leatherwork, brazing, marquetry and hand sewing...as well as the production methods of shaping, joining and finishing which gives the furniture its intrinsic qualities.

The Directional Collection offers the discriminating homemaker an unparalleled group of coordinated furniture designed to create an integrated, harmonious, contemporary environment.

See end sheets for color.

LEATHERS Many Directional tables and storage units are offered with leather tops, door fronts, and leather-lined trays and drawers. A choice of five hand-glazed leathers illustrated in the next column have been selected to coordinate with the wood finishes. Heavier gauge leathers are used for the interwoven seats of chairs 9001 and 9101, and are limited to cordovan, antique white, and saddle (not shown here).

MARBLE Roman Travertine, an imported Italian marble, and Radio Black, a domestic marble, have been chosen for the Directional units because they offer a richness of surface and provide the color-tone most desirable with the wood finishes and with the brass. White Carrara Glass not illustrated here, is also available for cabinet and table tops. This opaque, milky white glass is especially resistant to chipping and surface stains.

WOOD FINISHES Using the finest imported solid mahogany and mahogany veneers, the Directional Collection offers a variety of finishes: Saffron, Sandrift, Walnut, and Teak, illustrated on the facing page, and Black Lacquer, available as a standard finish, but not shown here. The Directional wood finishes have seven stages of application. These steps, most of which are by hand, create a distinctive quality that enhances the natural grain of the mahogany, producing a smooth and lustrous finish. Upholstery with exposed wood frames is available in four additional wood finishes not included in this chart; bisque, natural light walnut, cordovan mahogany and black. Due to the natural variations in wood grains, there may be color variations from the wood tones illustrated here.

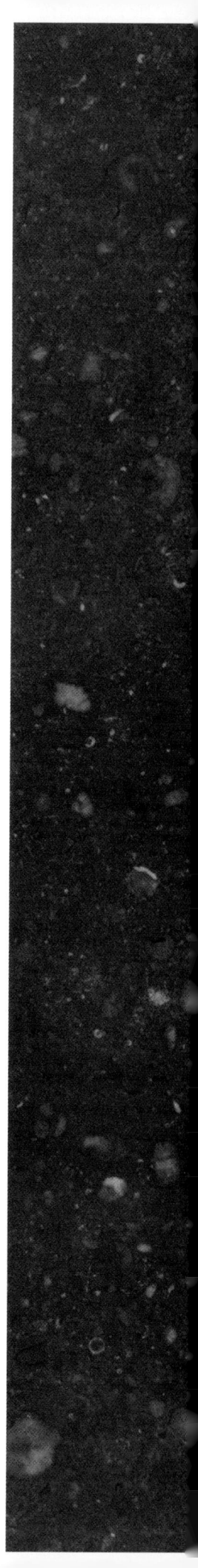

SAFFRON

SANDRIFT

WALNUT

TEAK

8206 72" CHEST, WALNUT FINISH, BRASS BASE / OPTIONAL TOPS AND WOOD BASE.

STORAGE

STORAGE / The storage units in the Directional collection are all illustrated in this section. These versatile designs provide multiplicity of possible uses for every function in today's home. The basic groups of chests and cabinets together with their related bookcases and storage tops extend a great variety of design interest. The overall coordination of the designs permits endless combinations individually suited to living room, dining room, bedroom or leisure areas as well as institutional use.

In addition, there are several units designed for specific storage needs such as bar cabinets, high men's dressers and double dressers. Some cabinets are also designed for hi-fidelity radio, phonograph and television custom installations.

Many storage units are available with wood or brass leg bases. Several storage units are available with wood, marble or white carrara glass tops. One group has inlaid leather tops and leather lined drawer bottoms color coordinated with the various wood finishes. Selection of coordinated wood finishes, leathers and marbles appears on pages 12 and 13.

One series is notable because its design allows a choice of many custom interior arrangements of trays and shelves. These cabinet chest combinations have alternate tops and bases. Included in the group is a selection of bookcases, room dividers and china storage units. A chart explaining these variations with specifications can be found on page 27.

OPPOSITE: **7306** 72" CABINET, SANDRIFT FINISH; BRASS BASE; SCREEN FOLD DOORS / ALTERNATE WOOD BASE; WOOD, MARBLE OR WHITE CARRARA GLASS TOP / INTERIOR FITTINGS SHOWN ON PAGE 27

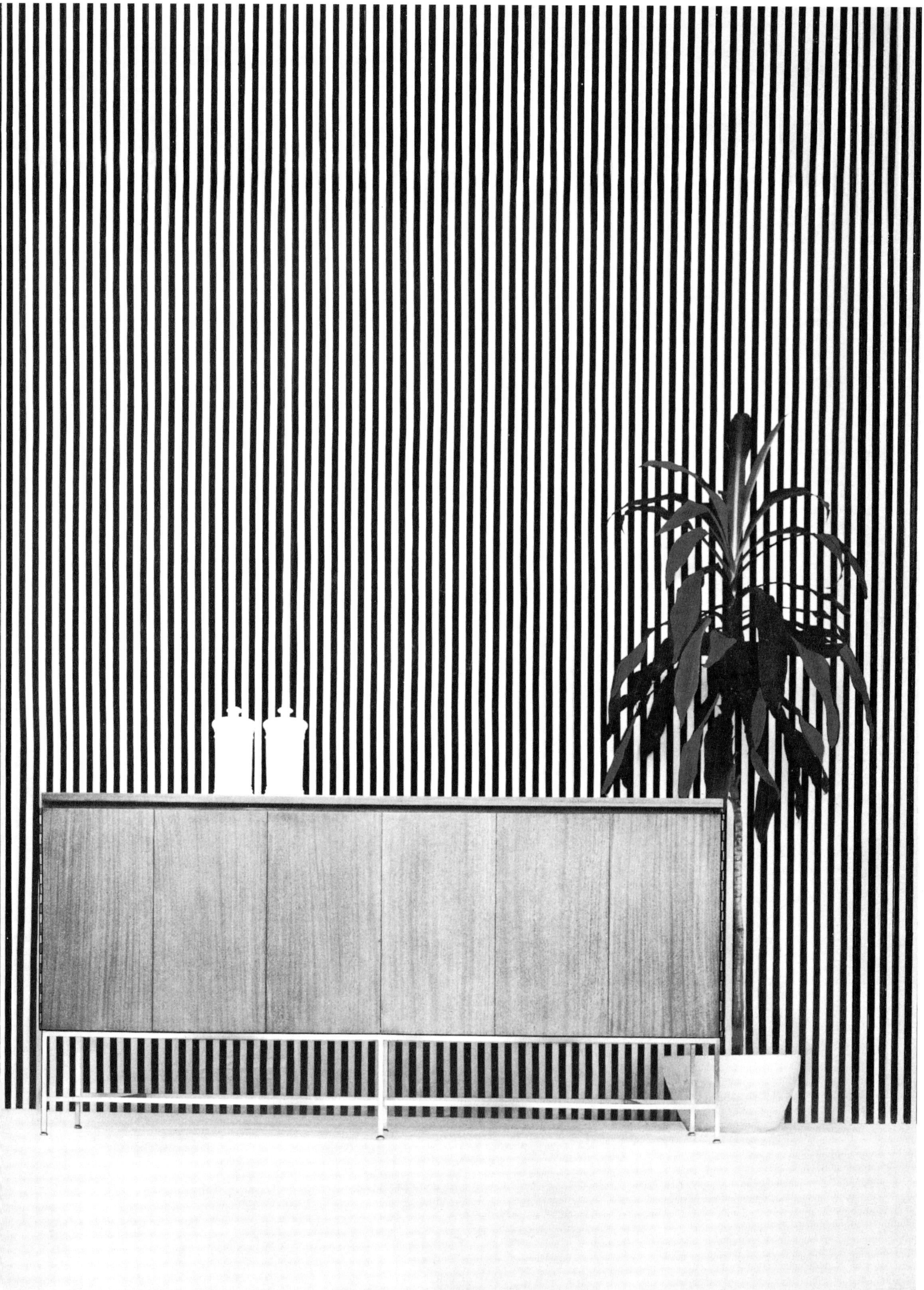

18

• **8506** 72" CABINET CHEST WITH **8006** BREAKFRONT SANDRIFT FINISH, BRASS BASE / 402 CHAIR.

• **8203** 36" CHEST, TEAK FINISH, WHITE CARRARA 140 BRASS PLANT STAND.

7303 36" CHEST WITH **7903** ROOMDIVIDER TOP, WALNUT FINISH, BRASS BASE AND FRAMING / AVAILABLE SEPARATELY / 1329 CHAIR.

7305 60" CHEST, TEAK FINISH, SCREENFOLD DOORS,
BRASS BASE / OPTIONAL TOPS, INTERIORS, BASE, PAGE 27.

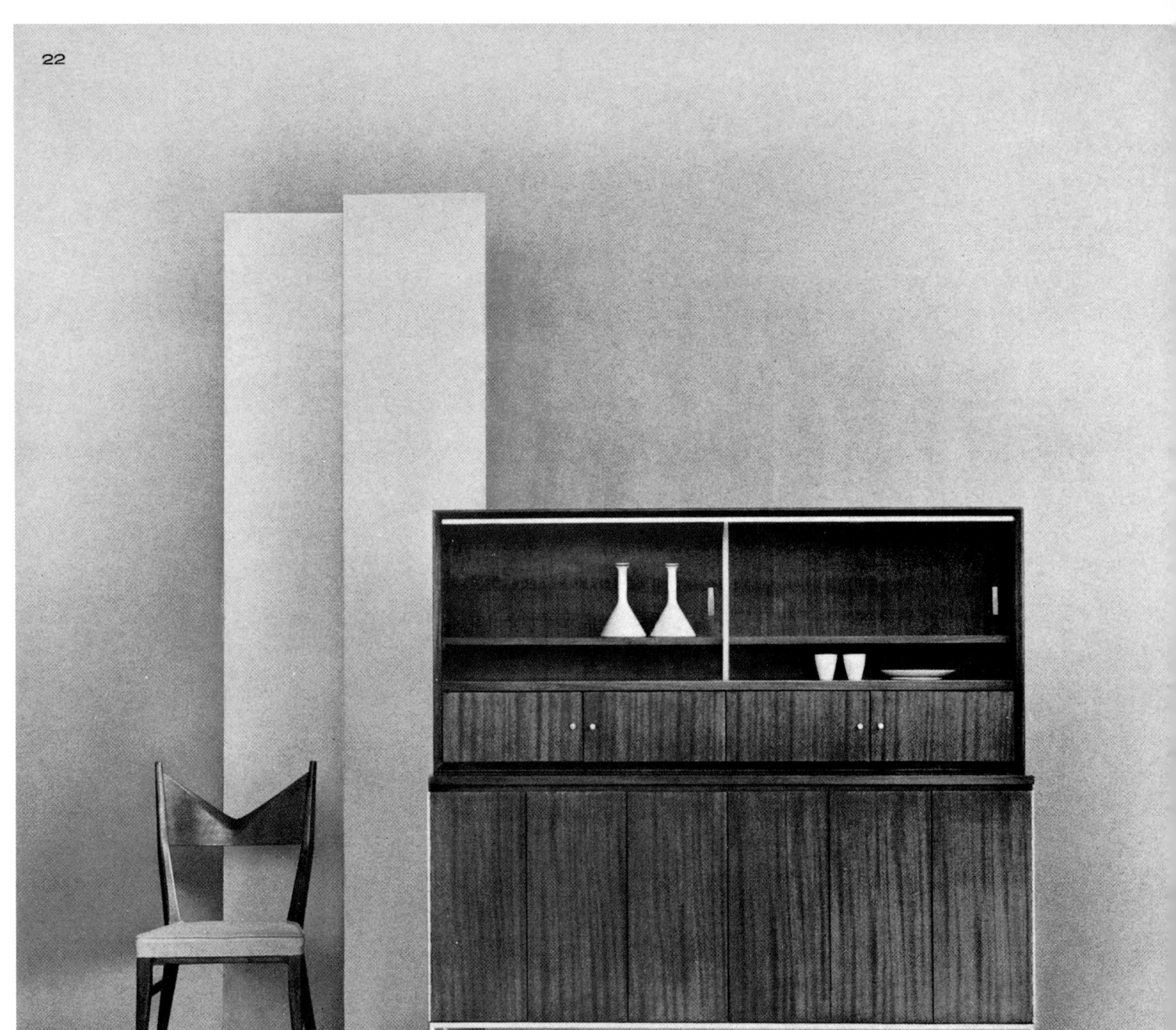

7305 60" CABINET WITH **7705** CHINA UNIT, WALNUT FINISH, BRASS BASE. CHINA UNIT HAS DOUBLE CABINET, ADJUSTABLE SHELF WITH SLIDING GLASS DOORS / OPTIONAL INTERIORS PAGE 27 / 1080 SIDE CHAIR.

8203 36" CHEST, WALNUT FINISH, BRASS BASE, WITH **7803** SECRETARY TOP, GLASS-BACKED CANED DOORS, ADJUSTABLE SHELVES INSIDE / 1320 CHAIR.

24

RIGHT: 7304 48" CABINET / **7804** CHINA UNIT, ADJUSTABLE SHELF WITH THREE DRAWERS, SLIDING GLASS DOORS.
BELOW: **7303** 36" CHEST, SANDRIFT FINISH, BRASS BASE / **7001** CHAIR / OPTIONAL INTERIORS, TOPS AND BASES SHOWN ON PAGE 27.

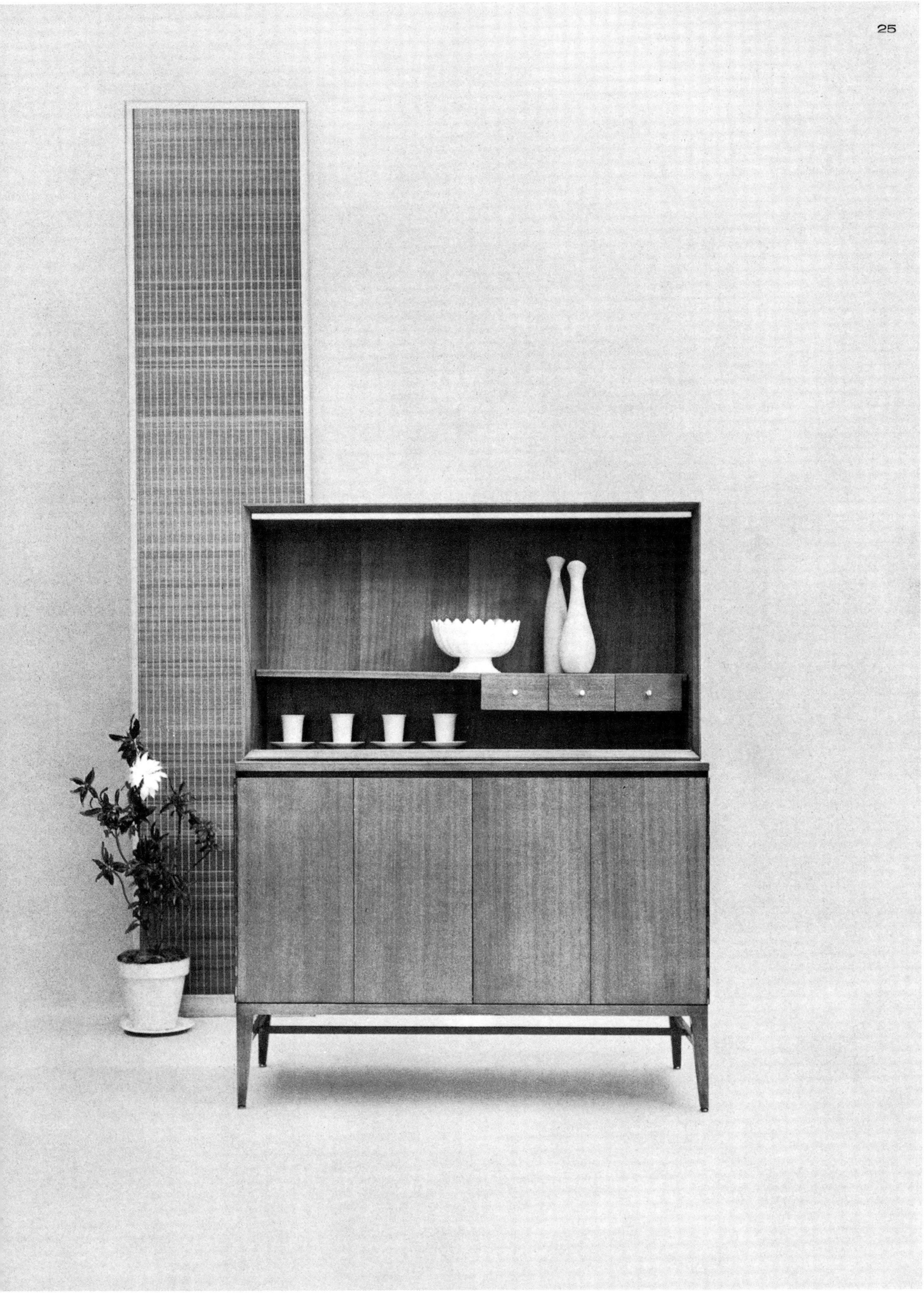

26

7303 36" CHEST WITH **1099**
SLIDING GLASS DOORS (NOT ILL
TRATED) ADJUSTABLE SHELF.

7304 48" CHEST, SCREENF
DOORS, WOOD BASE / 1094 TABLE

27

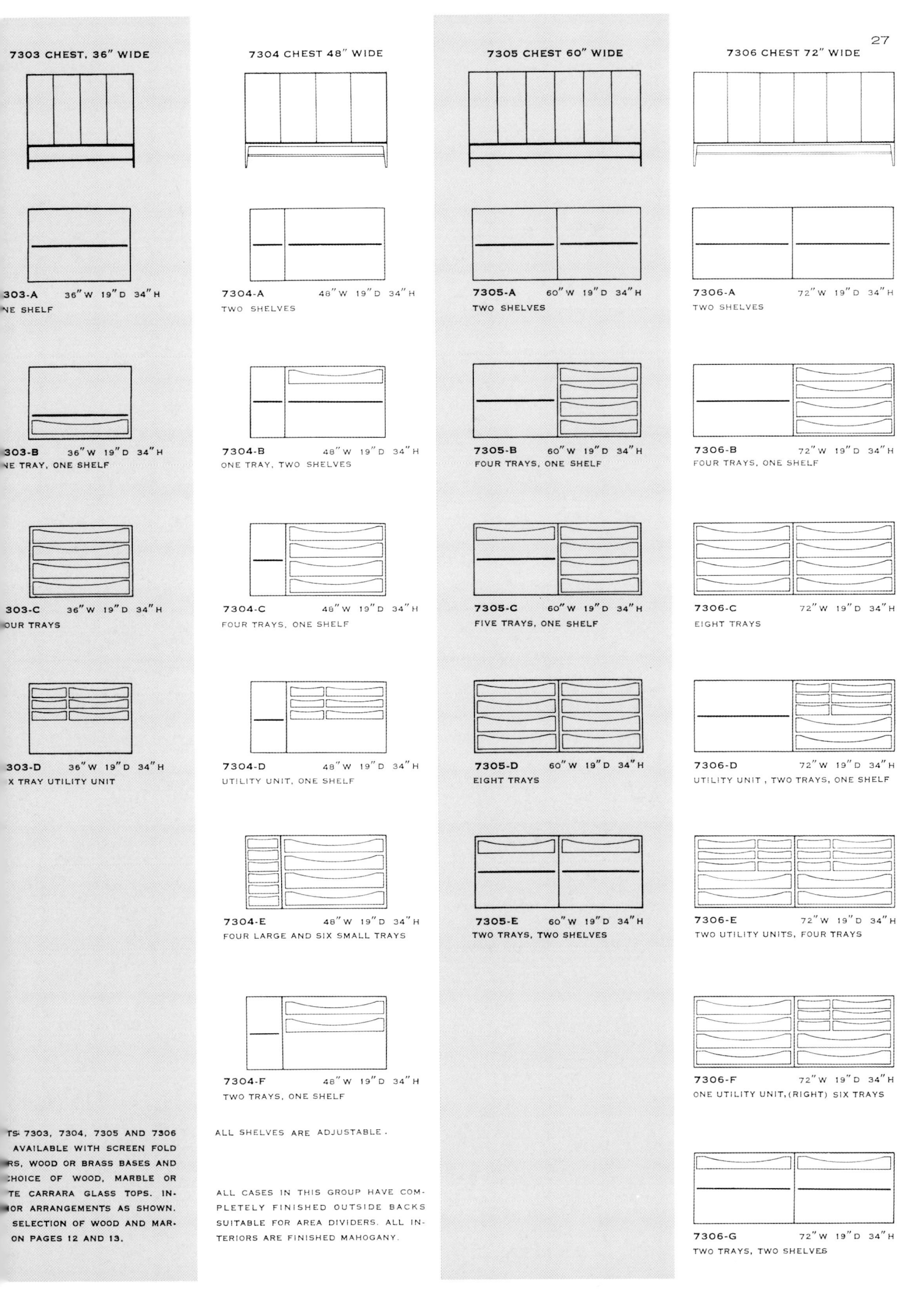

7303 CHEST, 36" WIDE	7304 CHEST 48" WIDE	7305 CHEST 60" WIDE	7306 CHEST 72" WIDE
7303-A 36"W 19"D 34"H ONE SHELF	7304-A 48"W 19"D 34"H TWO SHELVES	7305-A 60"W 19"D 34"H TWO SHELVES	7306-A 72"W 19"D 34"H TWO SHELVES
7303-B 36"W 19"D 34"H ONE TRAY, ONE SHELF	7304-B 48"W 19"D 34"H ONE TRAY, TWO SHELVES	7305-B 60"W 19"D 34"H FOUR TRAYS, ONE SHELF	7306-B 72"W 19"D 34"H FOUR TRAYS, ONE SHELF
7303-C 36"W 19"D 34"H FOUR TRAYS	7304-C 48"W 19"D 34"H FOUR TRAYS, ONE SHELF	7305-C 60"W 19"D 34"H FIVE TRAYS, ONE SHELF	7306-C 72"W 19"D 34"H EIGHT TRAYS
7303-D 36"W 19"D 34"H SIX TRAY UTILITY UNIT	7304-D 48"W 19"D 34"H UTILITY UNIT, ONE SHELF	7305-D 60"W 19"D 34"H EIGHT TRAYS	7306-D 72"W 19"D 34"H UTILITY UNIT, TWO TRAYS, ONE SHELF
	7304-E 48"W 19"D 34"H FOUR LARGE AND SIX SMALL TRAYS	7305-E 60"W 19"D 34"H TWO TRAYS, TWO SHELVES	7306-E 72"W 19"D 34"H TWO UTILITY UNITS, FOUR TRAYS
	7304-F 48"W 19"D 34"H TWO TRAYS, ONE SHELF		7306-F 72"W 19"D 34"H ONE UTILITY UNIT, (RIGHT) SIX TRAYS
			7306-G 72"W 19"D 34"H TWO TRAYS, TWO SHELVES

CHESTS 7303, 7304, 7305 AND 7306 ARE AVAILABLE WITH SCREEN FOLD DOORS, WOOD OR BRASS BASES AND A CHOICE OF WOOD, MARBLE OR WHITE CARRARA GLASS TOPS. INTERIOR ARRANGEMENTS AS SHOWN. SEE SELECTION OF WOOD AND MARBLE ON PAGES 12 AND 13.

ALL SHELVES ARE ADJUSTABLE.

ALL CASES IN THIS GROUP HAVE COMPLETELY FINISHED OUTSIDE BACKS SUITABLE FOR AREA DIVIDERS. ALL INTERIORS ARE FINISHED MAHOGANY.

7027 72" CABINET, FOR CUSTOM INSTALLATION OF TELEVISION AND HI-FIDELITY EQUIPMENT, LEATHER FRONT, SCREEN FOLD DOORS, BRASS INLAID LEG POSTS / 408 CHAIR.

7020 38" SECRETARY, CANE DOORS, PULL-OUT DESK SLIDE, BRASS STRETCHERS / 312 LOUNGE CHAIR / 7001 OCCASIONAL CHAIR.

7026 24" CABINET, **7023** 36" BAR CABINET, **7025** 24" CHEST, WALNUT FINISH, BRASS LEG POSTS / BAR HAS LIFT-UP TOP, WHITE MICARTA WELL / 402 CHAIR.

7706 72″ CHEST, LEATHER FRONT SCREENFOLD DOORS, INLAID BRASS EDGED TOP, BRASS LEGS, FITTED WITH THREE DRAWERS AND SIX TRAYS, LEATHER LINED / ALTERNATE BUFFET 7706-A / ALTERNATE TOPS AND WOOD BASE.

7704 48" MASTER CHEST, SCREENFOLD DOORS, LIFT-UP MIRRORED TOP, EQUIPPED WITH ELECTRIC SHAVER AND OUTLET, LEATHER-LINED DRAWERS AND GRADUATED TRAYS, PALLETS TO HOLD FORTY SHIRTS (SEE INSET).

7707 72" CHEST, CANED, PANELLED-BACK SCREENFOLD DOORS, WOOD OR LEATHER TOP WITH INLAID BRASS EDGE, EIGHT LEATHER-LINED TRAYS / ALTERNATE MARBLE OR WHITE CARRARA GLASS TOPS, WOOD OR BRASS BASE / AS BUFFET 7707-A, WITH TWO TRAYS, TWO SHELVES.

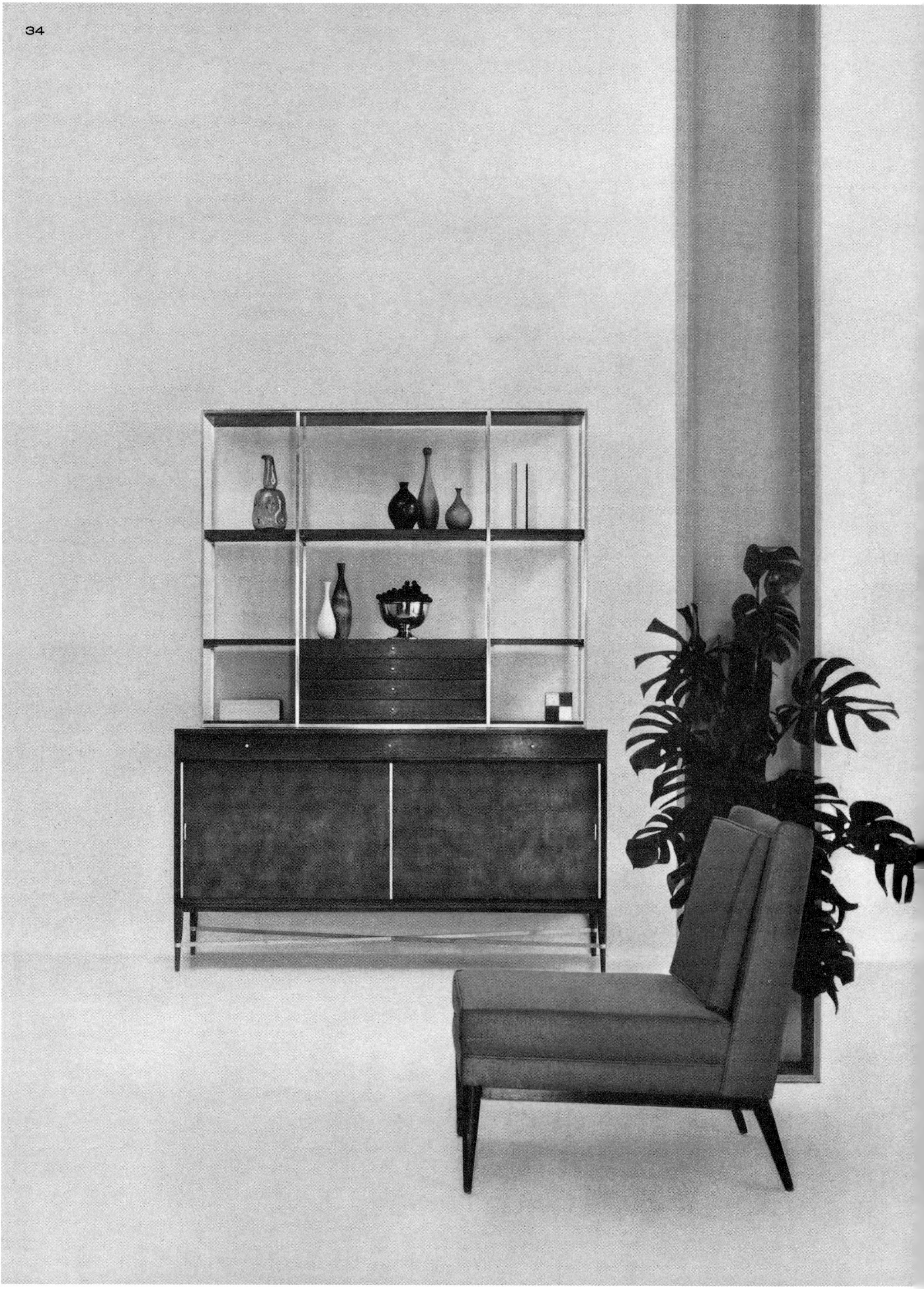

1006 66" CHEST, EIGHT DRAWERS; BRASS STRETCHERS.

)66 66" BUFFET CABINET WITH 1095 60" BREAKFRONT TOP. HAND-GLAZED LEATHER SLIDING DOORS;
TRETCHERS AND STRUCTURAL FRAMING, BRASS DOOR EDGES / AVAILABLE SEPARATELY / 300 CHAIR

1066 66" CABINET, THREE DRAWERS; STORAGE SPACE WITH ADJUSTABLE SHELVES, LEATHER SLIDING DOORS, BRASS STRETCHERS AND DOOR EDGES.

LEFT: **1003** 36", CHEST, FIVE DRAWERS, BRASS STRETCHERS.

BELOW: **1013** 36" HIGH CHEST. SEVEN DRAWERS PLUS FOUR TRAYS BEHIND DROP-LID FRONT, BRASS STRETCHERS / 1306 STOOL.

1070 DINING TABLE, BRASS STRETCHER BASE, 38X60" EXTENDS TO 84" / 1080 CHAIRS.

DINING

DINING / The Directional collection offers a wide selection of dining room furniture. The tables in this section range from small extension tables suitable for dinette or leisure rooms, to large formal dining tables. Also included in this group are several drop-leaf extension tables which when closed are compact wall units that extend up to 128 inches and seat up to twelve people.

The dining chairs illustrated with these tables include armless side chairs and arm chairs. Some of the outstanding design features in these chairs are the cane backs, interwoven leather seats and upholstered seats and backs of foam rubber. The wood parts are available in coordinated finishes. These chairs are explained in more detail in the seating section, page 77.

Dining room storage units - chests, cabinets and china units - are illustrated in the storage section, page 15.

Buffet servers and tea carts are illustrated in the occasional furniture section page 47.

OPPOSITE: **7028** OVAL DINING TABLE, TOP 41" W 62" D, OPENS T 128". TOP HAS BRASS INLAID EDGE; BRASS STRETCHERS / 7001 CHAIRS

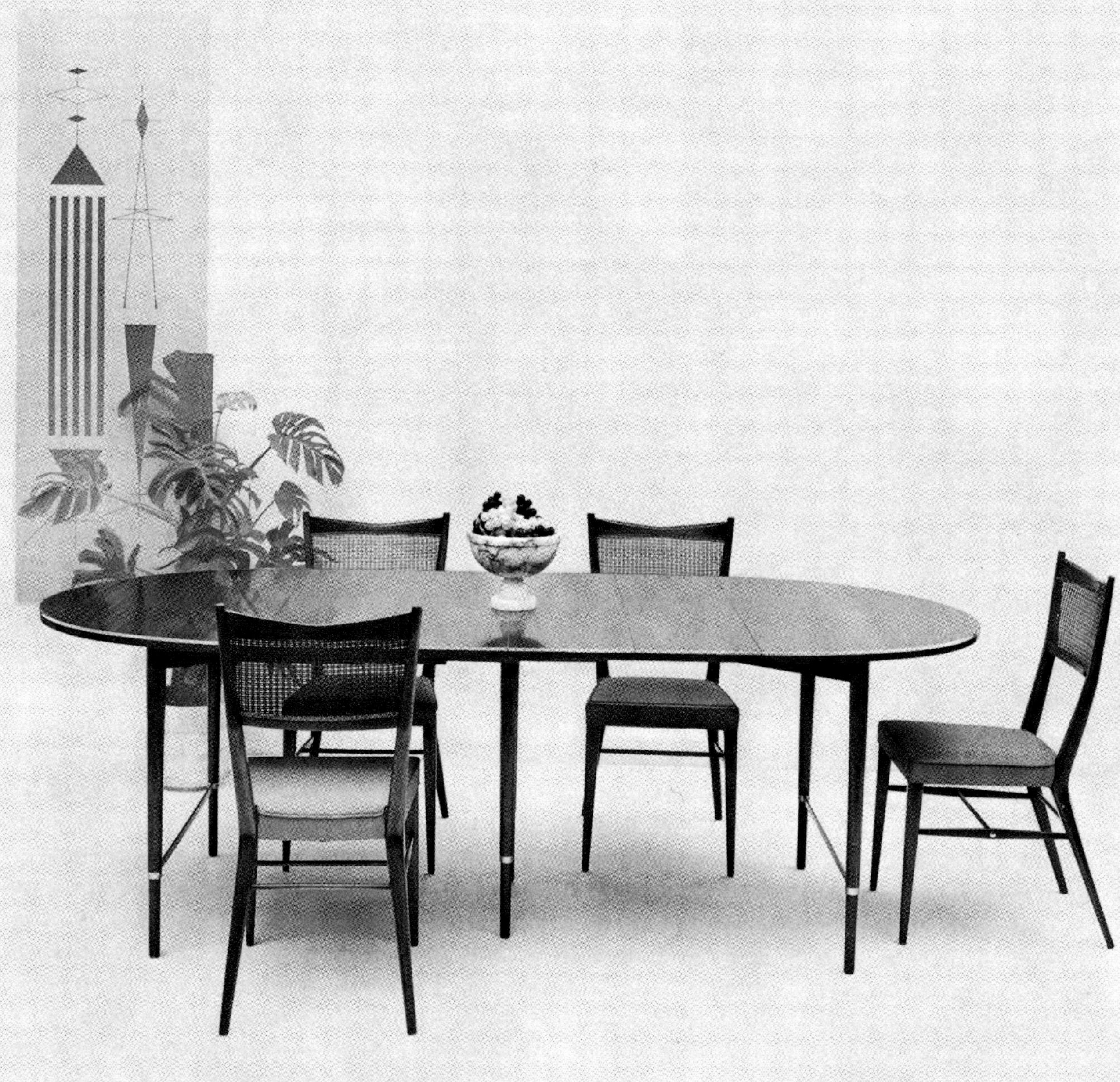

8907 ROUND DINING TABLE, 48" DIAMETER, OPENS TO 72", BRASS STRETCHERS, / 9002 LEATHER SIDE CHAIR / 9102 ARMCHAIR.

8905 DINING TABLE, TOP 36" W 54" D, OPENS TO 78", BRASS STRETCHERS / 9002 LEATHER CHAIR.

ABOVE: **8909** DINING TABLE, TOP 72"W 40"D; EXTENDS TO 102". BRASS STRETCHERED STATIONARY BASE / 9001 UPHOLSTERED SIDE CHAIR; 9101 ARMCHAIR.
OPPOSITE, TOP: **7017** OVAL DROPLEAF DINING TABLE, TOP 21½"W 40"D; WITH LEAVES UP 47". EXTENDS TO 91". BRASS-EDGED TOP; BRASS STRETCHERS / 7001 CHAIR.
OPPOSITE, BOTTOM: **1071** DROPLEAF DINING TABLE, TOP 40"W 20"D, WITH LEAVES UP 50", EXTENDS TO 86" / 1080 SIDE CHAIR.

45

9315 60" CONSOLE SERVER, BRASS FRAME, / ALTERNATE WOOD, MARBLE, WHITE CARRARA GLASS TOP.

OCCASIONAL FURNITURE AND TABLES

OCCASIONAL FURNITURE AND TABLES / The group in this section provides the interesting and functional accent pieces needed to complement any living area. This selection includes game tables, console tables, coffee tables, serving carts, corner tables, lamp tables, end tables and room dividers as well as other occasional pieces. They offer a great variety of design interest in the use of material, detail, size and scale, to fit any contemporary interior. Several tables feature caned shelves and inlaid leather tops. The selection of wood, marble, glass and leather for tops is illustrated on pages 12 and 13.

OPPOSITE: **7004** GAME TABLE, TOP 36"W 20"D; WITH INLAID MACASSAR EBONY CHESS BOARD. BACKGAMMON BOARD SPECIAL ORDER. FELT LINED STORAGE COMPARTMENT; BRASS STRETCHER / 7001 CHAIR.

49

7003 CARD TABLE, 34" SQUARE. MAHOGANY AND MACASSAR EBONY INLAY TOP WITH BRASS EDGE, SINGLE DRAWER, BRASS STRETCHER / 7001 CHAIR.

ROOM DIVIDER WITH **7905** SHELF AND DRAWER UNIT ON **9305** LOW BASE. 60″ WIDE, BRASS STRUCTURAL FRAMING / 9305 BASE MAY BE USED AS COFFEE TABLE WITH ALTERNATE TOPS.

ABOVE: **9313** 40" SMALL SERVER, TWO DRAWERS AND OPEN SHELVES, BRASS FRAME/ALTERNATE WOOD, MARBLE, OR WHITE CARRARA GLASS TOP.

RIGHT: **7504** 48" CONSOLE SERVER, FOUR DRAWERS AND CANED SHELF, BRASS FRAME/ALTERNATE WOOD, MARBLE, OR WHITE CARRARA GLASS TOP.

OPPOSITE LEFT: **7011** 54" CONSOLE TABLE, TWO DRAWERS, BRASS EDGED TOP, BRASS STETCHER.

OPPOSITE RIGHT: **1096** 60" CONSOLE SERVER, OPEN SHELVES, BRASS FRAME.

53

56

LEFT: **1094** CIGARETTE TABLE, 20" DIAMETER. BRASS BASE; WHITE CARRARA GLASS TOP.

RIGHT: **7006** END TABLE, BRASS X STRETCHER, 18" W 26" D / **7007** LAMP TABLE WITH BRASS FRAMED GLASS SHELF, 24" W 30" D / **7008** TRIPOD PEDESTAL TABLE 22" DIAMETER / **7005** COFFEE TABLE, TWO DRAWERS, BRASS STRETCHERS, 54" W 20" D

8715 COFFEE TABLE, TOP 60" W 24" D, AND **8713** CIRCULAR COFFEE TABLE, 42" DIAMETER. BRASS FRAMES / ALTERNATE WOOD, MARBLE OR WHITE CARRARA GLASS TOP.

8703 LOW DISPLAY TABLE, 48" X 36", AND **8704** HIGH DISPLAY TABLE, 48" X 18".
BRASS BASES, WHITE CARRARA GLASS TOPS / AVAILABLE WITH ¾" MARBLE TOPS.

7015 COMMODE, TOP 32" W 28" D, THREE DRAWERS, INLAID BRASS EDGED TOP / **7012** LAMP TABLE, TOP 32" W 26" D, BRASS EDGED LEATHER INLAID TOP, SINGLE DRAWER, BRASS FRAME, GLASS SHELF.

62

ABOVE: **8735** PLATEAU CORNER OR COFFEE TABLE, TOP 54" W 32" D. SINGLE DRAWER, WOOD SHELF.

OPPOSITE, TOP: **8738** MAGAZINE TABLE, TOP 22" W 28" D. THREE CANED SHELVES / E-8 LAMP.
BOTTOM, LEFT: **8731** END TABLE, TOP 24" W 28" D. TWO DRAWERS, CANED SHELF.
BOTTOM, RIGHT: **8736** END TABLE, TOP 20" W 24" D. SINGLE DRAWER, TWO CANED SHELVES / 7001 CHAIR.

8734 ROUND SIDE TABLE, 32" DIAMETER, BRASS EDGE, CANED SHELF / AVAILABLE WITH WOOD OR LEATHER TOP / 1329 CHAIR / LAMP E-10.

8739 COFFEE TABLE, TOP 60" W 20" D, BRASS EDGE, THREE DRAWERS, OPEN EITHER SIDE, CANED SHELF / AVAILABLE WITH WOOD OR LEATHER TOP.

7014 WEDGE TABLE, 24″ W 26″ D, SINGLE DRAWER, GLASS SHELF WITH BRASS FRAME / **7018** ROUND COFFEE TABLE, 42″ DIAMETER, WOOD OR MARBLE TOP, BRASS STRETCHERS / **7016** CORNER TABLE, 32″ SQUARE. ANGLE TIER, TWO DRAWERS.

8722 END TABLE, TOP 28" W 24" D; WOOD TOP ON BRASS BASE / **8702** LAMP TABLE, TOP 24" W 28" D; WOOD TOP, SHELF AND SINGLE DRAWER ON BRASS BASE / **8732** SQUARE OCCASIONAL TABLE, TOP 20" SQUARE (**1093**, SQUARE CORNER TABLE, TOP 32" SQUARE, NOT SHOWN) WHITE CARRARA GLASS TOP ON BRASS BASE / TABLES SHOWN ARE AVAILABLE WITH CHOICE OF WOOD, MARBLE OR WHITE CARRARA TOPS.

9403 BRASS HEADBOARD, 6'6" FOR TWO TWIN BEDS. UPHOLSTERED OR WOOD FINISHED PANELS / 8712 NIGHT TABLES / 7709 BENCH.

BEDROOM

BEDROOM / Designs in this section include headboards, night tables, dressing tables and benches. These designs dramatically display the combination of refinement and function resulting in outstanding examples of contemporary design.

All Directional bedroom storage pieces may be found in the storage section. Note that these storage pieces have optional interior arrangements that are particularly suited for bedroom use, see page 15. Refer to the seating portions of this book for other appropriate upholstered seating pieces for the contemporary bedroom, which are on page 77.

Headboards illustrated are shown in the 6'6" size for two twin beds, but are also available in the 3'3" single twin size, 4'6" double and 5'0" king size.

OPPOSITE: **7002** 44" DRESSING TABLE WITH LIFT UP TOP, WHITE GLASS MAKE-UP WELL; BRASS EDGED TOP BRASS STRETCHERS / **7010** VANITY STOOL, CANE SEAT, LOOSE FOAM RUBBER CUSHION / **5018** CHAISE LOUNGE

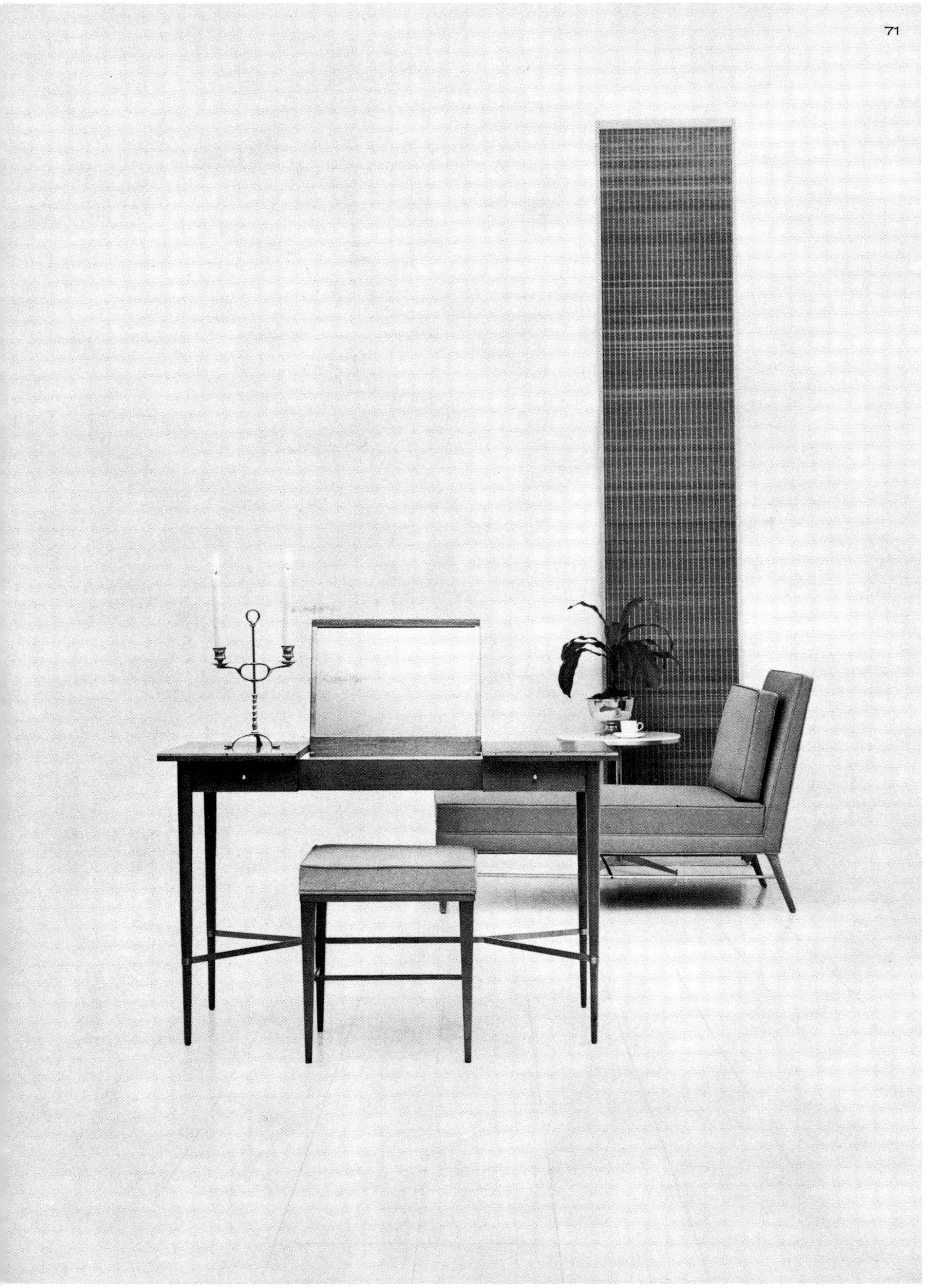

7703 CANE HEADBOARD, 6'6" FOR TWO TWIN BEDS. CANE PANELS ARE PROJECTED FROM SOLID BACKBOARD ON BRASS PINS / 7700 NIGHT TABLE.

1052 HEADBOARD, 6'6" FOR TWO TWIN BEDS. WOOD OR UPHOLSTERED PANELS SET IN WOOD FRAME / 1047 NIGHT TABLE.

74

OPPOSITE TOP:

8712 NIGHT TABLE, TOP 20" W 24" D. TWO DRAWERS, BRASS FRAME / ALTERNATE WOOD, MARBLE OR WHITE CARRARA GLASS TOP.

1047 NIGHT TABLE, TOP 21" 22" D. PULL-OUT WOOD SHELF BRASS SLIDE, WOOD STRETCHER.

OPPOSITE BOTTOM:

7700 NIGHT TABLE, TOP 22" W 20" D. SINGLE DRAWER AND STORAGE COMPARTMENT, WOOD OR LEATHER TOP WITH INLAID BRASS EDGE / ALTERNATE MARBLE OR WHITE CARRARA GLASS TOP / E-9 VANITY LAMP.

8714 NIGHT TABLE, TOP 20" 20" D. TWO DRAWERS, CAN SHELF, BRASS FRAME / ALTERN WOOD, MARBLE OR WHITE CARRA GLASS TOP.

7708 VANITY, TOP 52" W 22" D. LIFT-UP MIRROR TOP, SIX DRAWERS / **7709** 30" BRASS BENCH. CANE SEAT WITH SNAP-ON FOAM RUBBER CUSHION.

75

1307 SOFA 81", LOOSE-CUSHION SEAT AND BACK, WOOD BASE / 1094 CIGARETTE TABLE.

SEATING

SEATING / The Directional seating collection offers a wide range of seating units for both home and institutional use. Simplicity of design, refined detailing and proper scaling make this collection outstanding in its capability to complement any contemporary interior.

The individual seating category of lounge and pull-up chairs retains a design continuity that creates a refined dimensional quality from every viewing angle.

Smaller occasional chairs for dining, desk and card tables shown are an important part of this collection. Some with leather and cane detail are considered to be among the most notable examples of this type of seating in contemporary furniture design.

All Directional seating is upholstered in foam rubber with densities especially engineered to each particular seating requirement. Several units are offered with a choice of either down or foam rubber back cushions. Directional Showrooms display a wide and carefully selected group of coordinated fabrics. Customers may submit their own material for custom covering.

The selection of wood finishes is on page 13.

OPPOSITE: SEATING GROUP WITH 50" **5004-L** LEFT ARM LOVESEAT, AND 77" **5006-R** RIGHT ARM SOFA. LOOSE-CUSHION SEAT AND BACK, BRASS STRETCHERS / 8705-R PLATEAU TABLE / 8706 COFFEE TABL

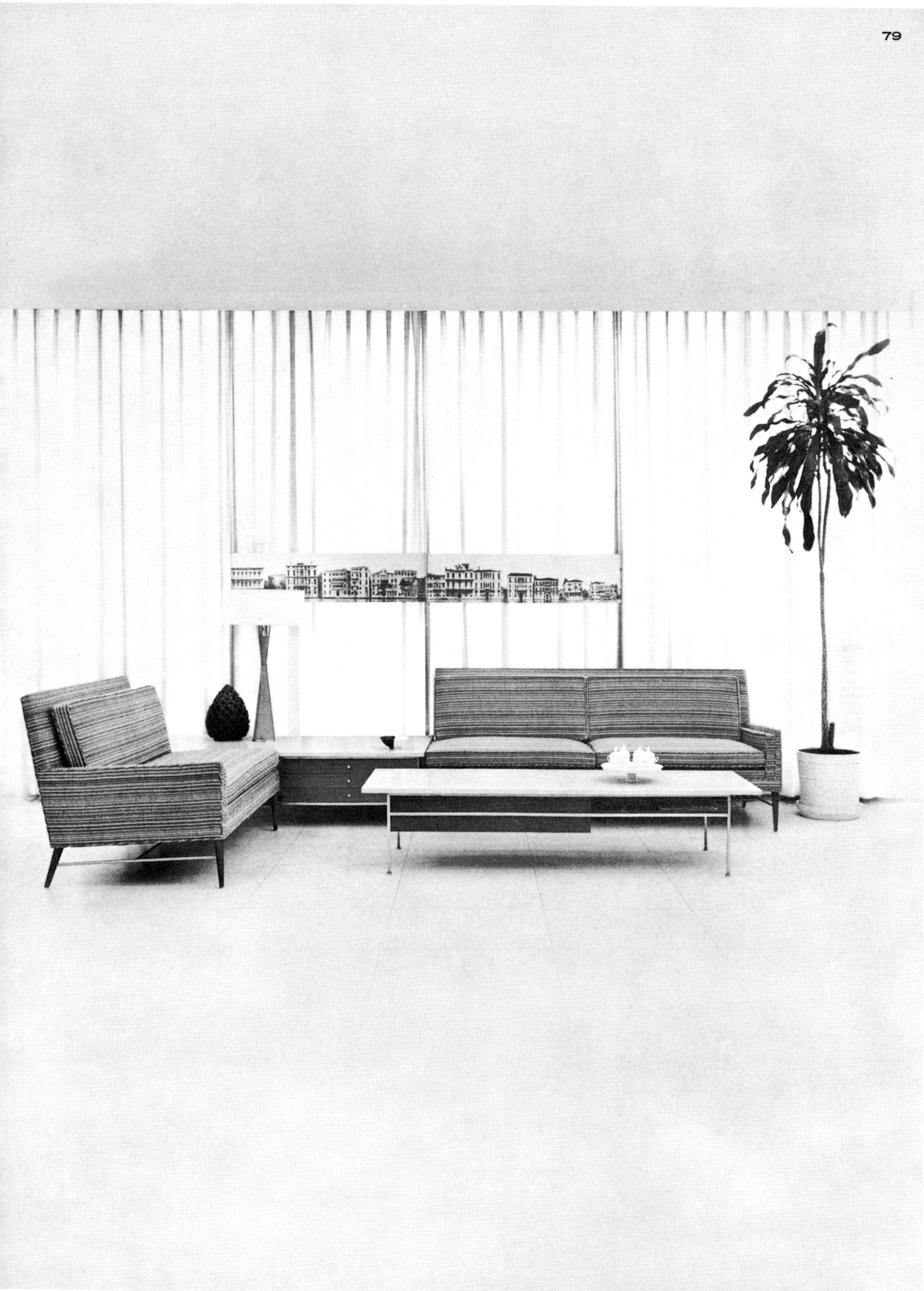

80

ABOVE: **5018** CHAISE LOUNGE, LOOSE BACK CUSHION, BRASS STRETCHER.

LEFT: **5012** ARMCHAIR, SET-IN ARM DETAIL, BRASS STRETCHER / **5000** ARMLESS CHAIR, LOOSE-CUSHION SEAT AND BACK, BRASS STRETCHER.

RIGHT: **1306** 20″ ALL-ROUND SQUARE, BRASS X-STRETCHER BASE.

82

302 ARMCHAIR / **1312** HIGH BACK CHAIR / **300** ARMLESS CHAIR.

ALL PIECES SHOWN ON THESE TWO PAGES HAVE WOOD FRAMED BASE, LOOSE BACK CUSHIONS. 1300 SERIES HAS LOOSE SEAT CUSHIONS, 300 SERIES HAS TIGHT SEATS.

314 HIGH BACK CHAIR WITH WEDGE SHAPED BACK CUSHION, LOOSE SEAT CUSHION / **314** MATCHING OTTOMAN.

303½ ARMLESS LOVESEAT.

OPPOSITE: **1327** 96" SOFA, FOAM RUBBER SEAT AND ARM CUSHIONS, DOWN FILLED BACK PILLOWS, WALNUT BASE / 8732 TABLE.
BELOW: **1321** OPEN ARM LOUNGE CHAIR, WALNUT FRAME, LOOSE BACK PILLOW / 1094 CIGARETTE TABLE.

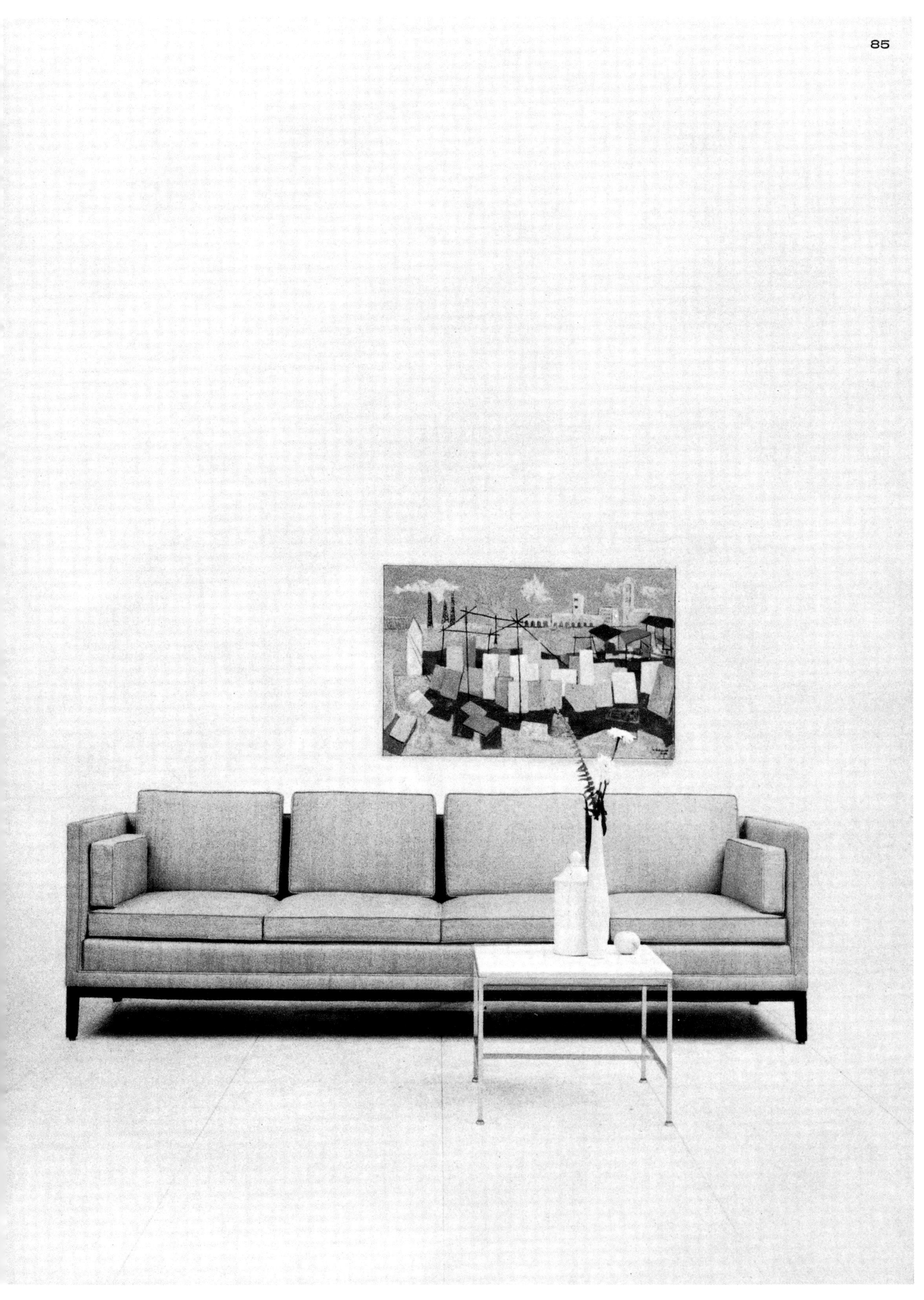

RIGHT: **1320** ARMLESS LOUNGE CHAIR, WALNUT FRAME / 1094 CIGARETTE TABLE.
BELOW: **1329** HIGH-BACK WING CHAIR, LOOSE BACK PILLOW, WALNUT FRAME.

BELOW: **1322** LOUNGE CHAIR, LOOSE SEAT CUSHION, WALNUT FRAME / TWO **8704** DISPLAY TABLES.

LEFT: **1323** LOUNGE CHAIR, LOOSE-CUSHION SEAT AND DOWN BACK, WALNUT FRAME BASE.
RIGHT: **2002** LOUNGE CHAIR, LOOSE-CUSHION SEAT, WOOD FRAME BASE / **2010** OTTOMAN WITH MATCHING BASE.

LEFT: **1328** PULL-UP CHAIR, SCULPTURED WALNUT ARMS / **7006** TABLE.
RIGHT: **2015-L** 76" DEN BED WITH BACK, ONE-PIECE FOAM RUBBER SEAT, REMOVABLE. WEDGE CUSHIONS / **8734** ROUND TABLE / **E-11** FLOOR LAMP.

89

8026-R 84", RIGHT TUXEDO-ARM SOFA, LOOSE BACK CUSHIONS, ONE PIECE SEAT, BRASS LEG BASE / 7015 COMMODE / 7006 TABLE / E-5 TABLE LAMP.

8046-R 84", HALF BACK SOFA WITH **8018-L** 76", ROOM DIVIDER SOFA, FORMS OPEN ANGLE SEATING GROUP, BRASS LEG BASE / 8713 COFFEE TABLE.

8000 CENTER CHAIR
30"W 33"D 27½"H

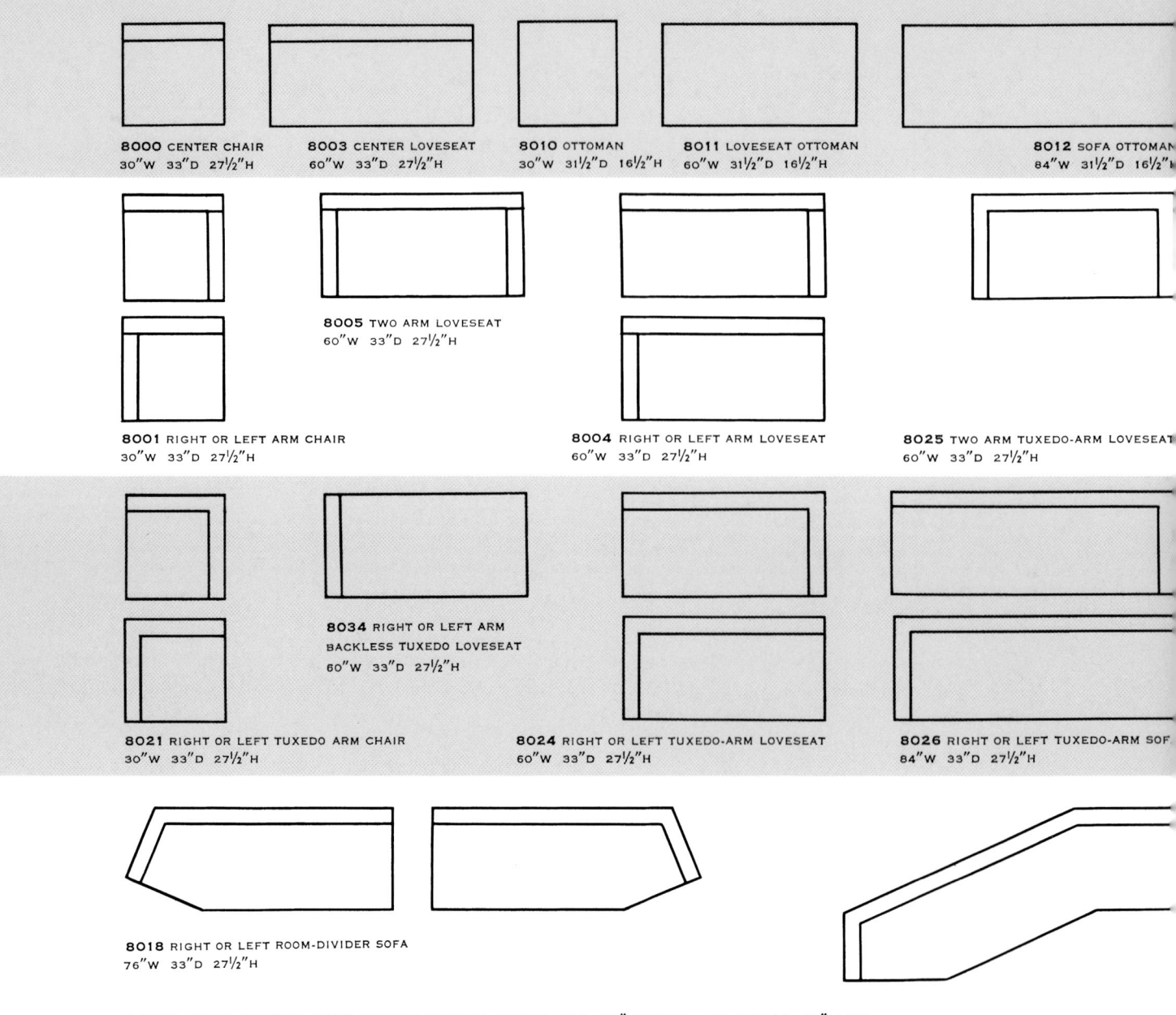

8003 CENTER LOVESEAT
60"W 33"D 27½"H

8010 OTTOMAN
30"W 31½"D 16½"H

8011 LOVESEAT OTTOMAN
60"W 31½"D 16½"H

8012 SOFA OTTOMAN
84"W 31½"D 16½"H

8005 TWO ARM LOVESEAT
60"W 33"D 27½"H

8001 RIGHT OR LEFT ARM CHAIR
30"W 33"D 27½"H

8004 RIGHT OR LEFT ARM LOVESEAT
60"W 33"D 27½"H

8025 TWO ARM TUXEDO-ARM LOVESEAT
60"W 33"D 27½"H

8034 RIGHT OR LEFT ARM BACKLESS TUXEDO LOVESEAT
60"W 33"D 27½"H

8021 RIGHT OR LEFT TUXEDO ARM CHAIR
30"W 33"D 27½"H

8024 RIGHT OR LEFT TUXEDO-ARM LOVESEAT
60"W 33"D 27½"H

8026 RIGHT OR LEFT TUXEDO-ARM SOFA
84"W 33"D 27½"H

8018 RIGHT OR LEFT ROOM-DIVIDER SOFA
76"W 33"D 27½"H

SEATING GROUP SHOWING **8017** QUARTER-OCTAGON CORNER SOFA, 72" SQUARE, AND **8046-L** 84" LEFT HALF-BACK ARMLESS SOFA, LOOSE BACK CUSHIONS, ONE PIECE SEAT, BRASS BASE / **8017-T** TRIANGLE FILLER TABLE, FITS CORNER BEHIND 8017 QUARTER-OCTAGON / **8732** SQUARE TABLE / **E-1** TABLE LAMP.

8006 CENTER ARMLESS SOFA
84"W 33"D 27½"H

8007 TWO ARM SOFA
84"W 33"D 27½"H

8036 RIGHT OR LEFT ARM BACKLESS TUXEDO SOFA
84"W 33"D 27½"H

8006 RIGHT OR LEFT ARM SOFA
84"W 33"D 27½"H

8046 RIGHT OR LEFT HALF-BACK ARMLESS SOFA
84"W 33"D 27½"H

8056 RIGHT OR LEFT ARM HALF-BACK SOFA
84"W 33"D 27½"H

8027 TUXEDO-ARM SOFA
84"W 33"D 27½"H

8066 RIGHT OR LEFT TUXEDO ARM HALF-BACK SOFA
84"W 33"D 27½"H

THE METRIC GROUP OF UPHOLSTERED UNITS WAS SPECIFICALLY DEVELOPED TO SATISFY ANY GROUP SEATING DEMANDS. THE BASIC UNITS, ILLUSTRATED IN THIS CHART PROVIDE INNUMERABLE MODULAR SEATING ARRANGEMENTS. THE UNITS MAY BE ORDERED TO ANY LENGTH AND ARE OFFERED WITH EITHER BRASS OR WOOD BASES.

8019 RIGHT OR LEFT ANGLE CORNER SOFA
33"D 27½"D • WALL LENGTHS 102" X 54"

8017 QUARTER OCTAGON CORNER SOFA
33"D 27½"D • WALL LENGTHS 72" X 72"

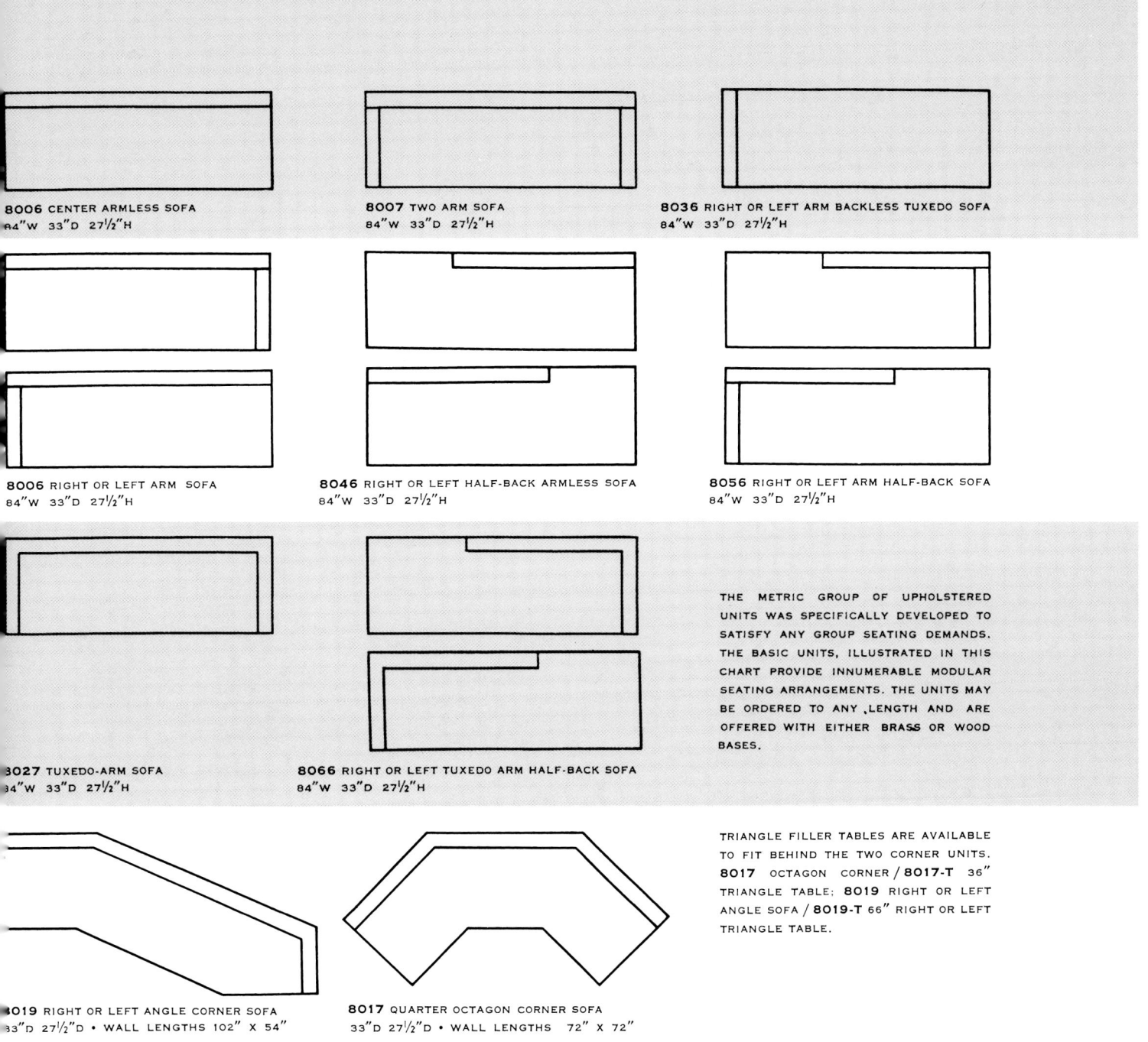

TRIANGLE FILLER TABLES ARE AVAILABLE TO FIT BEHIND THE TWO CORNER UNITS. **8017** OCTAGON CORNER / **8017-T** 36" TRIANGLE TABLE; **8019** RIGHT OR LEFT ANGLE SOFA / **8019-T** 66" RIGHT OR LEFT TRIANGLE TABLE.

8006-R 84" RIGHT ARM SOFA, LOOSE BACK CUSHIONS, ONE PIECE SEAT, WOOD LEGS / 8731 END TABLE / E-4 TABLE LAMP.

94

407 84" SOFA, FOAM RUBBER SEAT, DOWN OR FOAM RUBBER CUSHIONS, SOLID WALNUT FRAME / 8732 TABLE.

400 ARMLESS CHAIR / **409** PULL-UP ARM CHAIR, WALNUT FRAMES.

96

LEFT: **402** WOOD ARM LOUNGE CHAIR, LOOSE CUSHION, WALNUT FRAME.

RIGHT: **7019** DINING CHAIR / **7001** SIDE C
7009 ARM CHAIR / **7024** DINING ARM CHAIR
SHOWN). ALL HAVE SCULPTURED MAHOGANY FR
CANED BACKS, UPHOLSTERED SEATS.

97

1080 SIDE CHAIR / **1082** ARM CHAIR, SOLID MAHOGANY SHAPED FRAME, UPHOLSTERED SEAT.

9101 UPHOLSTERED ARM CHAIR / **9001** UPHOLSTERED SIDE CHAIR, SOLID MAHOGANY FRAME, BRASS STRETCHERS / **9002** SIDE CHAIR / **9102** ARM CHAIR, WOVEN LEATHER SEAT AND SHAPED LEATHER BACK, SOLID MAHOGANY FRAME.

8804 54" TABLE DESK, CENTER DRAWER, PULL-OUT SLIDES AT EACH END, BRASS FRAME / ALTERNATE WOOD, MARBLE OR WHITE CARRARA GLASS TOPS / 7009 CHA

DESKS

DESKS / These Directional desks are designed to satisfy every work or study requirement of the home, particularly in the living room, library or bedroom. Several are equally suited for small offices and reception areas. Coordinated desk chairs are shown in the seating section page 77.

Desks are shown with wood tops but several are available with marble or glass. See selection illustrated on pages 12 and 13.

An extensive collection of executive office desk units designed by Paul McCobb is illustrated in a separate catalog.

OPPOSITE: **7021** 66" DOUBLE PEDESTAL DESK, BACK PANEL, BRASS EDGED TOP, BRASS STRETCHERS PULL-OUT SLIDE, SEVEN DRAWERS INCLUDING FILE DRAWER. / 7009 CANE BACK OCCASIONAL CHAIR

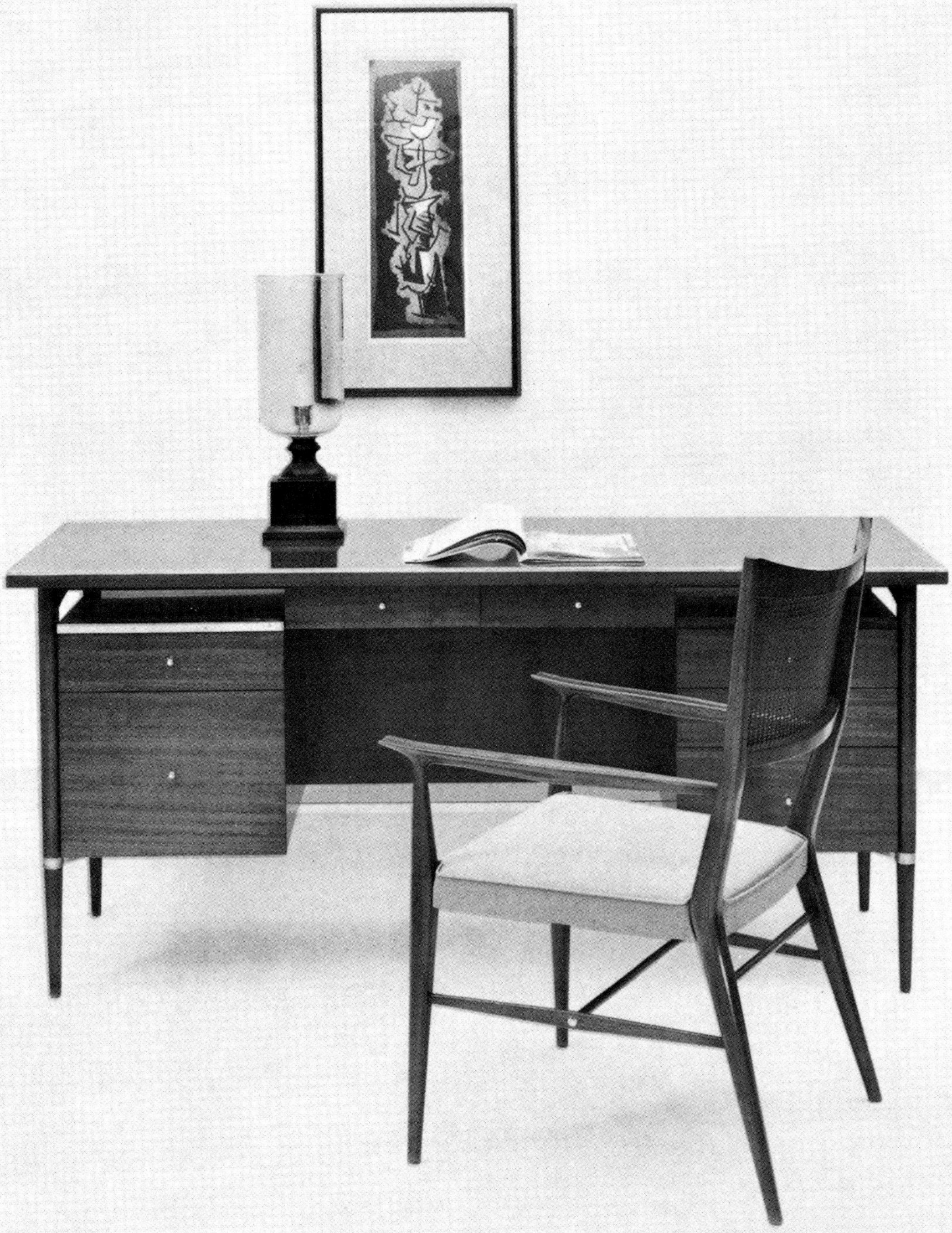

7022 42" LADY'S DESK. BRASS EDGED TOP, THREE DRAWERS, FOUR UPPER DRAWERS, BRASS STRETCHER / 7019 CHAIR.

TOP: **1090** 54" DESK, THREE DRAWERS INCLUDING FILE DRAWER, BRASS STRETCHER / 1082 CHAIR / 2010 BRASS DESK LAMP.
BOTTOM: **7000** 56" DESK, FOUR DRAWERS INCLUDING FILE DRAWER, PULL-OUT WRITING SHELF, BACK PANEL, BRASS EDGED TOP, BRASS STRETCHERS / 7009 CHAIR.

WOOD UNITS   SPECIFICATIONS

WOOD used in all chests, cabinets and tables illustrated in this catalog is specially selected imported solid mahogany or mahogany veneer, properly aged and kiln dried.

CABINET designs are carefully engineered incorporating the most advanced methods of assembly and construction in the joining, gluing, veneering and edge banding. Top quality inspected materials are used in all cabinets and tables. All of the time honored techniques in cabinet work are used; tables and chairs are mortise and tenoned or doweled, drawers use tongue and grooved or dove-tailed construction, post-and-panel and panel-to-panel joints are tongued or doweled. All units are corner blocked for additional strength wherever necessary. The construction of these units is guaranteed against defects in normal use.

FINISHES employ scientifically proven ingredients, formulae and application techniques, that afford the utmost protection against changing climatic conditions and normal wear. These transparent finishes are hand-rubbed to a dull satin luster, revealing the true wood character and graining. Finishes are heat and moisture resistant under normal use, but cannot be guaranteed against abuse, scratching, excessive heat or solvents. For the protection of these finishes we recommend the sparing use of white wax, lightly applied, and briskly rubbed with a soft cloth in the direction of the wood grain. Over-polishing destroys the lustrous satin finish created especially for these designs.

BRASS used in these pieces is solid brass rod or tubing, with a scientifically developed protective transparent metal lacquer finish, and only requires dusting with a soft, clean cloth. The use of polish or abrasives will penetrate the finish and cause eventual discoloration.

LEATHER used is genuine top grain leather with hand glazed finish. Occasional use of saddle soap for cleaning will keep this leather pliant and strong, retaining its original appearance.

MARBLE used is the finest quality imported Roman Travertine and domestic Radio Black. The White Carrara glass used is especially resistant to chipping and surface stains. Both materials may be cleaned with mild soap suds. Abrasive cleaners will spoil the finish. Special waxes and cleaners are available to protect the marble and remove stains.

UPHOLSTERY UNITS

WOOD exposed on upholstered units is either solid mahogany, maple or walnut. Concealed frames are a combination of elm and solid white maple, which are the strongest hardwoods available suitable for frame construction.

FRAMES are engineered for utmost strength using glued, doweled and screwed construction, corner-blocked for greater rigidity.

SPRINGING methods vary with the individual unit and include hand-tied coil springs, interwoven rubber webbing, and other springing techniques especially developed for these designs. Construction is unconditionally guaranteed in normal use.

CUSHIONING materials used in upholstered units are selected densities of molded and sheet foam rubber, with additional cotton felt, and curled hair as specified. Fabric upholstered over rubber is taped to the edges, providing a non-slip construction which retains the original shape of the cushion. Finished tailoring is achieved through hand-sewing and hand-fitting, assuring perfection of detail in design execution.

Index and Value Guide

PRICING

The prices shown herein reflect what it is believed the items would ng in excellent condition on average, as of the date of publication, if sold a first-class auction gallery specializing in modern design. The range is ended to reflect options for each piece, e.g., marble top vs. glass top. xcellent condition" means, for purposes of this guide, original condition h only gentle aging and very minor normal wear. Deductions should be de for more than normal wear and/or damage. Reupholstery or other onditioning is only acceptable if it is of the quality of the original. Adjust- ments should also be made for local demand, e.g., prices in Manhattan or Los Angeles are likely to be higher than in smaller or more conservative markets. As of the date of publication, prices are rising rapidly as demand is increasing. Whether this trend will continue cannot be predicted. Although the photographs are of complete items, e.g., cabinet with bookcase top, the price refers to the description in the index, which in some cases is only one part.

STORAGE

NUMBER	DESCRIPTION	VALUE	PAGE
03	CHEST, 36"W, 19"D, 36"H	$500-700	37
06	CHEST, 66"W, 19"D, 36"H	$800-1000	35
13	HIGH CHEST, 36"W, 19"D, 53"H	$700-900	37
66	CABINET, 66"W, 19"D, 36"H	$700-900	36
95	BRASS BREAKFRONT TOP, 60"W, 14"D, 48"H	$500-700	34
99	SMALL CHINA UNIT, 36"W, 13"D, 24"H	$200-300	26
20	SECRETARY DESK, 38"W, 18"D, 77"H	$1200-1400	29
23	BAR UNIT, 36"W, 18"D, 34"H	$400-600	30
25	CHEST, 24"W, 18"D, 34"H	$400-600	30
26	CABINET, 24"W, 18"D, 34"H	$400-600	30
27	CABINET SUITABLE FOR TELEVISION, HI-FI, ETC., 72"W, 25"D, 36"H	$600-800	28
03	CHEST, 36"W, 19"D, 34"H **B I T**	$600-800	24
04	CHEST, 48"W, 19"D, 34"H **B I T**	$600-800	26
05	CHEST, 60"W, 19"D, 34"H **B I T**	$1000-1400	21
06	CHEST, 72"W, 19"D, 34"H **B I T**	$1000-1400	17
04	MASTER HIGH CHEST, 48"W, 19"D, 50"H **L**	$1200-1400	32
05	CHINA CABINET TOP, 60"W, 14"D, 26"H	$900-1200	22
06	LEATHER DOOR CHEST, 72"W, 19"D, 34"H **B L**	$1200-1400	31
06-A	LEATHER DOOR CABINET, 72"W, 19"D, 34"H **B L**	$1200-1400	31
07	CANED FRONT CHEST, 72"W, 19"D, 34"H **B L**	$900-1100	33
07-A	CANED FRONT CABINET, 72"W, 19"D, 34"H **B L**	$900-1100	33
03	TALL CABINET TOP, 36"W, 13"D, 48"H	$500-700	23
04	CHINA UNIT TOP, 48"W, 14"D, 26"H	$200-300	25
03	OPEN FRAME BOOKCASE UNIT, 36"W, 13"D, 36"H	$400-500	20
06	BREAKFRONT TOP, 72"W, 19"D, 49"H	$600-800	18
03	CHEST, 36"W, 19"D, 34"H **B T**	$600-800	19

Y: **B**—SPECIFY WOOD OR BRASS; **F**—FABRIC TO BE SUPPLIED BY CUSTOMER; **I**—SPECIFY INTERIOR FITTINGS (SEE CHART ON PAGE 27); —SPECIFY LEATHER (SELECTION PAGE 12); **T**—SPECIFY WOOD, MARBLE OR WHITE CARRARA GLASS TOP (SELECTION PAGES 12 AND 13)

NUMBER	DESCRIPTION	VALUE	PAGE
8206	CHEST, 72"W, 19"D, 34"H **B T**	$800-1200	14
8506	CABINET BUFFET, 72"W, 19"D, 34"H **B T**	$800-1200	18

DINING TABLES

1070	EXTENSION TABLE, 60"W, 38"D, 29"H, EXTENDS TO 84" WITH TWO 12" LEAVES	$300-500	38
1071	DROP LEAF EXTENSION TABLE, 20"W, 40"D, 29"H CLOSED, 50"W, 40"D LEAVES UP, EXTENDS TO 86" WITH THREE 12" LEAVES	$300-500	45
7017	DROP LEAF TABLE, 21-1/2"W, 40"D, CLOSED, 47"W, 40"D LEAVES UP, EXTENDS TO 91" WITH FOUR 11" LEAVES	$300-500	45
7028	OVAL DINING TABLE, 62"W, 41"D, 29"H, EXTENDS TO 128" WITH SIX 11" LEAVES	$500-700	41
8905	DINING TABLE, 54"W, 36"D, 29"H, EXTENDS TO 78" WITH TWO 12" LEAVES	$300-500	43
8907	DINING TABLE, 48" DIAMETER, 29"H, EXTENDS TO 72" WITH TWO 12" LEAVES	$300-500	42
8909	DINING TABLE, 72"W, 40"D, 29"H, EXTENDS TO 102" WITH TWO 15" LEAVES	$600-800	44

DINING CHAIRS

1080	SIDE CHAIR, 18-1/4"W, 19-1/2"D, 34"H **F**	$100-200	98
1082	ARM CHAIR, 24"W, 24"D, 35"H **F**	$100-200	98
7001	SIDE CHAIR, 16-1/2"W, 19"D, 34-1/2"H **F**	$100-200	97
7009	ARM CHAIR, 23-3/4"W, 23"D, 36"H **F**	$100-200	97
7019	DINING CHAIR, 17-1/2"W, 21-1/4"D, 35-1/2"H **F**	$100-200	97
7024	ARM CHAIR, 23"W, 22"D, 36"H **F**	$100-200	97
9001	UPHOLSTERED SIDE CHAIR, 17-3/4"W, 20-1/2"D, 36"H **F**	$100-200	99
9002	SIDE CHAIR, LEATHER, 17-3/4"W, 21"D, 35-1/2"H **L**	$200-300	99
9101	UPHOLSTERED ARM CHAIR, 22"W, 20-1/2"D, 36"H **F**	$100-200	99
9102	ARM CHAIR, LEATHER, 22-1/2"W, 20-1/2"D, 35-1/2"H **L**	$250-350	99

OCCASIONAL FURNITURE AND TABLES

1072	ROLLING SERVER, 40"W, 20"D, 30"H (OPENS TO 80")	$350-450	54
1091	60" TABLE, 60"W, 19"D, 29"H	$400-500	55
1092	ROOM DIVIDER TOP, 60"W, 13"D, 60"H	$400-600	55
1093	CORNER TABLE, 32"W, 32"D, 16"H **T** (MARBLE, WHITE CARRARA GLASS ONLY) (NOT SHOWN)	$250-350	67
1094	CIGARETTE TABLE, 20"DIAMETER, 22"H (WHITE CARRARA GLASS ONLY)	$200-300	56
1096	CONSOLE SERVER, 60"W, 19"D, 16"H	$350-450	53
7003	CARD TABLE, 34"W, 34"D, 28-1/2" H	$400-500	50
7004	GAME TABLE, 36"W, 20"D, 28"H	$500-700	49
7005	COFFEE TABLE, 54"W, 20"D, 16-1/2"H	$400-500	57
7006	END TABLE, 18"W, 26"D, 18"H	$300-400	57
7007	LAMP TABLE, 24"W, 30"D, 22"H	$300-400	57
7008	ROUND PEDESTAL TABLE, 22"DIAMETER, 22"H	$250-350	57
7011	CONSOLE TABLE, 54"W, 18"D, 29"H	$250-350	53
7012	LEATHER TOP TABLE, 32"W, 26"D, 24"H	$300-400	61

JMBER	DESCRIPTION	VALUE	PAGE
14	WEDGE TABLE, 18"W AT FRONT, 24"W AT BACK, 26"D, 20"H	$200-300	66
15	COMMODE, 32"W, 28"D, 18"H	$250-350	61
16	CORNER TABLE, 32"W, 32"D, 22"H	$250-350	66
18	ROUND COFFEE TABLE, 42"DIAMETER, 16"H **T** (WOOD, MARBLE, ONLY)	$400-600	66
04	CONSOLE SERVER, 48"W, 19"D, 30"H **T**	$400-600	52
05	ROOM DIVIDER TOP, 60"W, 13"D, 60"H	$700-800	51
02	LAMP TABLE, 24"W, 28"D, 22"H **T**	$200-400	67
03	DISPLAY TABLE, 48"W, 36"D, 15"H **T** (MARBLE, WHITE CARRARA GLASS ONLY)	$400-600	60
04	DISPLAY TABLE. 48"W, 18"D, 22"H **T** (MARBLE, WHITE CARRARA GLASS ONLY)	$400-600	60
05	PLATEAU TABLE, 66"W, 32"D, 16"H **T**	$700-800	58
06	COFFEE TABLE, 72"W, 24"D, 15"H **T**	$400-600	58
13	ROUND COFFEE TABLE, 42"DIAMETER, 15"H **T**	$400-600	59
14	SIDE TABLE, 20"W, 20"D, 25"H **T**	$200-300	75
15	OBLONG COFFEE TABLE, 60"W, 24"D, 15"H **T**	$300-500	59
22	END TABLE, 28"W, 24"D, 20"H **T**	$150-250	67
31	END TABLE, 24"W, 28"D, 19"H **L T**	$250-350	62
32	OCCASIONAL TABLE, 20"SQ, 15"H **T**	$200-300	67
34	ROUND TABLE, 32"DIAMETER, 20"H **L T**	$150-250	64
35	PLATEAU TABLE, 54"W, 32"D, 16"H **L T**	$400-600	63
36	END TABLE, 20"W, 24"D, 19"H **L T**	$250-350	62
38	MAGAZINE SHELF TABLE, 22"W, 28"D, 20"H **L T**	$250-350	62
39	COFFEE TABLE, 60"W, 20"D, 16"H **L T**	$200-300	65
44	END TABLE, 18"W, 26"D, 18"H (NOT SHOWN) **L T**	$300-400	
03	SERVING CART, 36"W, 19"D, 29"H **T** (MARBLE, WHITE CARRARA GLASS ONLY)	$350-450	54
05	LOW BASE SERVER, 60"W, 19"D, 16"H **T**	$300-500	51
13	SMALL SERVER, 40"W, 16-1/2"D, 29"H **T**	$250-400	52
15	HIGH BASE SERVER, 60"W, 19"D, 29"H **T**	$300-500	46

:DROOM

47	NIGHT TABLE, 21"W, 22"D, 24"H	$150-200	75
50	39" UPHOLSTERED OR WOOD PANEL HEADBOARD, 37"H (NOT SHOWN, SEE 1052) **F**	$150-200	73
51	54" UPHOLSTERED OR WOOD PANEL HEADBOARD, 37"H (NOT SHOWN, SEE 1052) **F**	$150-200	73
52	78" UPHOLSTERED OR WOOD PANEL HEADBOARD, 37"H **F**	$200-300	73
02	DRESSING TABLE, 44"W, 18"D, 27-3/4"H	$300-400	71
10	VANITY BENCH, 16"W, 14"D, 17-1/2"H **F**	$100-150	71
00	NIGHT TABLE, 22"W, 20"D, 24"H **L T**	$200-300	75
01	39" CANED PANEL HEADBOARD, 39"H (NOT SHOWN, SEE 7703)	$200-300	72
02	54" CANED PANEL HEADBOARD, 39"H (NOT SHOWN, SEE 7703)	$200-300	72
03	78" CANED PANEL HEADBOARD, 39"H	$300-500	72
11	60" CANED PANEL HEADBOARD, 39"H, (NOT SHOWN, SEE 7703)	$300-400	72
08	DRESSING TABLE, 52"W, 22"D, 16-1/2"H	$300-400	74
09	VANITY BENCH, 30"W, 17-1/2"D, 16-1/2"H **F**	$150-250	74
2	NIGHT TABLE, 20"W, 24"D, 25"H	$200-300	75
4	NIGHT TABLE, 20"W, 20"D, 24"H **T**	$200-300	75

NUMBER	DESCRIPTION	VALUE	PAGE
9401	39" WOOD OR UPHOLSTERED PANEL HEADBOARD, 37"H (NOT SHOWN, SEE 9403) F	$100-200	68
9402	54" WOOD OR UPHOLSTERED PANEL HEADBOARD, 37"H (NOT SHOWN, SEE 9403) F	$100-200	68
9403	78" WOOD OR UPHOLSTERED PANEL HEADBOARD, 37"H F	$200-300	68
9404	60" WOOD OR UPHOLSTERED PANEL HEADBOARD, 37"H (NOT SHOWN, SEE 9403) F	$200-300	68

SEATING

300	ARMLESS CHAIR, 24"W, 30"D, 31"H F	$200-300	82
302	LOW ARM CHAIR, 27-1/2"W, 30"D, 31"H F	$300-400	82
303	ARMLESS LOW BACK LOVESEAT, 50"W, 30"D, 31"H (NOT SHOWN) F	$400-600	
303-1/2	ARMLESS HIGH BACK LOVESEAT, 50"W, 31"D, 34"H F	$300-500	83
304	RIGHT OR LEFT LOW BACK LOVESEAT, 52"W, 30"D, 31"H (NOT SHOWN) F		
307	SOFA, 81"W, 30"D, 31"H (NOT SHOWN, SEE 1307) F	$700-900	76
310	OTTOMAN, 27-1/2"W, 18"D, 15"H (NOT SHOWN) F	$100-200	
312	HIGH BACK CHAIR. 27-1/2"W, 31"D, 34"H (NOT SHOWN, SEE 1312) F	$300-400	82
314	HIGH BACK LOUNGE CHAIR, 30"W, 33"D, 41-1/2"H F	$400-500	83
314	OTTOMAN, 29"W, 18"D, 15"H F	$150-250	83
400	ARMLESS LOUNGE CHAIR, 24"W, 31-1/2"D, 34-1/2"H F	$300-400	95
402	WOOD ARM LOUNGE CHAIR, 26-1/2"W, 31"D, 34-1/2"H F	$400-500	96
407	SOFA, 83-1/2"W, 33-1/2"D, 32"H F	$1000-1200	94
408	ARMLESS OCCASIONAL CHAIR, 23-1/2"W, 30"D, 38"H (NOT SHOWN) F	$300-400	
409	OCCASIONAL WOOD ARM CHAIR, 26"W, 28-1/2"D, 35"H F	$400-500	95
412	TUB CHAIR, 26"W, 25"D, 31"H (NOT SHOWN) F	$400-500	
1300	ARMLESS CHAIR, 24"W, 30"D, 31"H (NOT SHOWN, SEE 300) F	$200-350	82
1302	LOW ARM CHAIR, 27-1/2"W, 30"D, 31"H (NOT SHOWN, SEE 302) F	$300-450	82
1303	ARMLESS LOVESEAT, 50"W, 30"D, 31"H (NOT SHOWN) F	$600-800	
1303-1/2	HIGH BACK ARMLESS LOVESEAT, 50"W, 31"D, 34"H (NOT SHOWN, SEE 303-1/2) F	$600-800	83
1304	RIGHT OR LEFT LOVESEAT, 52"W, 30"D, 31"H (NOT SHOWN) F	$400-500	
1306	ALL ROUND SQUARE, 20"W, 20"D, 16"H F	$200-250	81
1307	SOFA, 80"W, 30"D, 31"H F	$700-900	76
1312	HIGH BACK CHAIR, 28"W, 31"D, 34-1/2"H F	$300-400	82
1320	WOOD FRAME ARMLESS CHAIR, 24-1/2"W, 30"D, 32-1/2"H F	$300-400	86
1321	WOOD ARM LOUNGE CHAIR, 28"W, 31"D, 34"H F	$400-500	84
1322	WOOD FRAME UPHOLSTERED ARM CHAIR, 28-1/2"W, 30"D, 32-1/2"H F	$400-500	87
1323	LOOSE PILLOW BACK CHAIR, 30-1/2"W, 33"D, 32"H F	$300-400	88
1327	SOFA, 96"W, 33-1/2"D, 30-1/2H F	$800-1000	85
1328	WOOD ARM PULL-UP CHAIR, 27-1/2"W, 30-1/2"D, 35"H F	$300-400	88
1329	HIGH BACK WING CHAIR, 31"W, 32"D, 35"H F	$400-500	86
2002	LOUNGE CHAIR, 30"W, 35-1/2"D, 32"H F	$300-400	89
2010	OTTOMAN, 29"W, 21"D, 15"H F	$100-150	89
2015	RIGHT, LEFT OR TWO ARM DEN BED, 76"W, 33"D, 30"H (ARMLESS 74"W) F	$600-800	89
5000	ARMLESS CHAIR, 23-1/2"W, 35"D, 32"H F	$300-400	80
5001	RIGHT OR LEFT CHAIR, 27"W, 35"D, 32"H (NOT SHOWN)	$200-300	
5002	ARM CHAIR, 30-1/2"W, 35"D, 32"H (NOT SHOWN) F	$400-500	
5003	CENTER LOVESEAT, 50"W, 35"D, 32"H (NOT SHOWN) F	$400-500	

MBER	DESCRIPTION	VALUE	PAGE
)4	RIGHT OR LEFT LOVESEAT, 50"W, 35"D, 32"H **F**	$300-500	79
)5	TWO ARM LOVESEAT, 50"W, 35"D, 32"H (NOT SHOWN) **F**	$500-700	
)6	RIGHT OR LEFT SOFA, 77"W, 35"D, 32"H **F**	$600-800	79
)7	TWO ARM SOFA, 76"W, 35"D, 32"H (NOT SHOWN) **F**	$600-800	
12	ARM CHAIR, 25-1/2"W, 30"D, 37"H **F**	$250-350	80
15	RIGHT, LEFT OR TWO ARM DEN BED, 76"W, 32-1/2"D, 29-1/2"H (ARMLESS 74") (NOT SHOWN) **F**	$500-700	
18	CHAISE LOUNGE, 23"W, 54-1/2"D, 32-1/2"H **F**	$500-700	80
)0	CENTER CHAIR, 30"W, 33"D, 27-1/2"H (SEE CHART) **B F**	$200-300	92
)1	RIGHT OR LEFT ARM CHAIR, 30"W, 33"D, 27-1/2"H (SEE CHART) **B F**	$200-300	92
)2	ARM CHAIR, 30"W, 33"D, 27-1/2"H (SEE CHART) **B F**	$200-300	92
)3	CENTER LOVESEAT, 60"W, 33"D, 27-1/2"H (SEE CHART) **B F**	$300-400	92
)4	RIGHT OR LEFT ARM LOVESEAT, 60"W, 33"D, 27-1/2"H (SEE CHART) **B F**	$300-400	92
)5	TWO ARM LOVESEAT, 60"W, 33"D, 27-1/2"H (SEE CHART) **B F**	$300-400	92
)6	RIGHT, LEFT OR ARMLESS SOFA, 84"W, 33"D, 27-1/2"H **B F**	$400-500	93
)7	TWO ARM SOFA, 84"W, 33"D, 27-1/2"H (SEE CHART) **B F**	$500-700	92
0	OTTOMAN, 30"W, 31-1/2"D, 16-1/2"H (SEE CHART) **B F**	$100-200	92
1	LOVESEAT OTTOMAN, 60"W, 31-1/2"D, 16-1/2"H (SEE CHART) **B F**	$100-200	92
2	SOFA OTTOMAN 84"W, 31-1/2"D, 16-1/2"H (SEE CHART) **B F**	$100-200	92
7	QUARTER OCTAGON CORNER SOFA, 72"SQ, 33"D, 27-1/2"H **B F**	$200-300	92
8	RIGHT OR LEFT ROOM DIVIDER SOFA, 76"W, 33"D, 27-1/2"H **B F**	$500-700	91
9	RIGHT OR LEFT ANGLE CORNER SOFA, 105"PERIMETER, 33"D, 27-1/2"H (SEE CHART) **B F**	$300-400	92
21	RIGHT OR LEFT TUXEDO ARM CHAIR, 30"W, 33"D, 27-1/2"H (SEE CHART) **B F**	$200-300	92
22	TUXEDO ARM CHAIR, 30"W, 33"D, 27-1/2"H (SEE CHART) **B F**	$200-300	92
24	RIGHT OR LEFT TUXEDO ARM LOVESEAT, 60"W, 33"D, 27-1/2"H (SEE CHART) **B F**	$500-600	92
25	TWO ARM TUXEDO ARM LOVESEAT, 60"W, 33"D, 27-1/2"H (SEE CHART) **B F**	$500-600	92
26	RIGHT OR LEFT TUXEDO ARM SOFA, 84"W, 33"D, 27-1/2"H **B F**	$400-500	90
27	TUXEDO ARM SOFA, 84"W, 33"D, 27-1/2"H (SEE CHART) **B F**	$600-800	92
34	RIGHT OR LEFT TUXEDO ARM BACKLESS LOVESEAT, 60"W, 33"D, 27-1/2"H (SEE CHART) **B F**	$300-400	92
36	RIGHT OR LEFT TUXEDO ARM BACKLESS SOFA, 84"W, 33"D, 27-1/2"H (SEE CHART) **B F**	$300-400	92
46	RIGHT OR LEFT HALF-BACK ARMLESS SOFA, 84"W, 33"D, 27-1/2"H (54" BACK)	$300-400	91
56	RIGHT OR LEFT ARM HALF-BACK SOFA, 84"W, 33"D, 27-1/2"H (SEE CHART) **B F**	$300-400	92
)6	RIGHT OF LEFT TUXEDO ARM HALF-BACK SOFA, 84"W, 33"D, 27-1/2"H (SEE CHART) **B F**	$300-400	92
17-T	TRIANGLE TABLE (TO FIT BEHIND 8017 CORNER UNIT), 36"W, 26"D, 27-1/2"H	$200-300	92
19-T	TRIANGLE TABLE (TO FIT BEHIND 8019 RIGHT OR LEFT CORNER UNIT), 63"W, 24"D, 27-1/2"H	$200-300	92

:SKS

)0	DESK, 54"W, 26"D, 29"H	$500-700	105
)0	DESK, 56"W, 25"D, 29"H	$600-800	105
?1	DOUBLE PEDESTAL DESK, 66"W, 28"D, 29"H	$700-900	103
?2	LADY'S DESK, 42"W, 24"D, 34"H	$600-800	104
)4	TABLE DESK, 54"W, 28"D, 29"H **T**	$500-700	100

CREDITS

Designed by_____Paul McCobb

Art Direction and   Mollie Rogers McCobb
Graphic Work by   John W. Sheehan

Photographs for
Directional by_____Tom Yee

LEATHERS Many Directional tables and storage units are offered with leather tops, door fronts, and leather-lined trays and drawers. A choice of five hand-glazed leathers illustrated in the next column have been selected to coordinate with the wood finishes. Heavier gauge leathers are used for the interwoven seats of chairs 9001 and 9101, and are limited to cordovan, antique white, and saddle (not shown here).

MARBLE Roman Travertine, an imported Italian marble, and Radio Black, a domestic marble, have been chosen for the Directional units because they offer a richness of surface and provide the color-tone most desirable with the wood finishes and with the brass. White Carrara Glass not illustrated here, is also available for cabinet and table tops. This opaque, milky white glass is especially resistant to chipping and surface stains.

WOOD FINISHES Using the finest imported solid mahogany and mahogany veneers, the Directional Collection offers a variety of finishes: Saffron, Sandrift, Walnut, and Teak, illustrated on the facing page, and Black Lacquer, available as a standard finish, but not shown here. The Directional wood finishes have seven stages of application. These steps, most of which are by hand, create a distinctive quality that enhances the natural grain of the mahogany, producing a smooth and lustrous finish. Upholstery with exposed wood frames is available in four additional wood finishes not included in this chart; bisque, natural light walnut, cordovan mahogany and black. Due to the natural variations in wood grains, there may be color variations from the wood tones illustrated here.

STRAW GLAZE

SANDRIFT

SAFFRON

WALNUT

TEAK

ROMAN TRAVERTINE